Neville Goddard's

By Jeff Johnson

While every precaution has been taken in the preparation of this book, the publisher assumes no responsibility for errors or omissions, or for damages resulting from the use of the information contained herein.

NEVILLE GODDARD'S SUCCESS STORIES

First edition. June 20, 2023.

Copyright © 2023 Jeff Johnson.

ISBN: 979-8223869696

Written by Jeff Johnson.

Table of Contents

Joseph and Wilhelmina Goddard 1
Victor Goddard 10
You Are In Barbados! 16
Catherine Goddard 28
Neville 39
Famous People 50
That which I have done, I have done! Do nothing! 59
Friends 72
Stories from the Audience 110
Also by Jeff Johnson 118

"So when you see anyone in the world and you are going through—don't analyze yourself and ask, what have I done that is wrong? What have I done that is wrong? Well go to Scripture and find out. "He consigned me to disobedience," so if I disobey the Law, it is He. Then who is He? My own wonderful Lord. And who is that Lord? My imagination. That is the Father. That is the Lord. That is the Master.

So I obeyed him every moment of time; and when he took me up as a boy and shipped me two thousand miles away to school without any friends, any relatives to receive me, because the fire was so intense and the urge to go, I had to get going. And when I was fired from one job, or was fired from the other, or when I quit, I had that intense desire to do something that was different. It was He who was guiding me all along.

It was He who took me to London when I really wasn't qualified to do it; and then in London to find a man—a retired engineer who liked the psychic world and introduced me to this way of thinking—just a little spark—it was all there. He only had to put the spark to it; so when I came back, I was living in the second-hand bookstores in New York City. When I could afford a book, I'd buy a book. And when I traveled as a dancer, I traveled with my library. When the others played cards through the day to kill the time between shows—for we did three or four shows a day—I was reading my books. And when they went out after the show at night doing some things, I would take my books, and I built my library that way when I could ill afford to buy a book. That's the way I spent my money."

Lecture - Consigned To Disobedience April 23, 1971 - Neville

Introduction

I have researched over three hundred lectures by Neville Goddard regarding the Law. I include his personal success stories along with his family, friends, and audience. I use the same story more than once if there are additional details, but I only try to use two at the most with a couple of exceptions. I included the background of some of the people who are mentioned in the stories if I found information about them.

Joseph and Wilhelmina Goddard

Joseph N. Goddard (11/24/1874 - 10/31/1959) and Wilhemina Goddard (3/2/1880 - 10/24/1941) were Neville Goddard's parents. Neville talks about his mother making the Goddard name important to her children and eventually it became a very important name in Barbados. In the July 25, 1968 lecture *Awake O Sleeper* he said, "I know, in my own case, my family had really no financial, social, intellectual or any other background of mention, but my mother did not allow her ten children to know that. And if any of us did anything that Mother —well, she wasn't exactly ashamed of it, but she thought it could be better, and it was something that we really should not have done, she would then say to us, "Have you forgotten that you are a Goddard?" She made the name important. It had no importance whatsoever, but she made it important. So, she treated us as though we as a family were important. The result is that she lived long enough to see her family grow into importance in the community, all pulling their weight and being very important in their community.

Now, you can start it with any family in this world and treat the family as though they were important. Unfortunately, our parents think they are doing the right thing when they compare us to a neighbor and find us wanting. "Why can't you be like So-and-So?" Right away it implies you are not as good as – and, so, if that's the seed she is planting for the child, the child has to do that. But if you will take any child, and then – not flatter it, no – but in your mind's eye see it as important, and treat it in your mind's eye as though it were. See it successful."

Six days before that on July 19, 1968 in the lecture *Live In The End* Neville said, "And, then, with that assumption – and if you have children, I hope you do – well, then, instill that into the child. Instill it into all within the environment, and have them feel important.

I have no background, judged by human standards – either intellectual, financial or these things – we made it. But Mother instilled in us, when we did something of which she was ashamed she would say to us, "Have you forgotten that you are a Goddard?" Well, we didn't know. That must have been very important, because Mother said, "Have you forgotten that you're a Goddard?"

Well, I never heard that we had any background, but all of a sudden you begin to feel that you must be important. So, Mother instilled it into our mind's eye. She made the name important, so today it is important. Where we are, in the business sense, in every sense, it's important; but Mother did that, and she married a man who had no background, and took his name, but she made it important."

Neville talks about his father and his brother Victor's morning routine having inner conversations to start the day. In the lecture *Order Your Conversations Aright* he said, "But now let me share with you a story I know well, the story of my father. He was born a very poor white man in the Island of Barbados. My mother was born poor. She had nothing; he had nothing. And they proceeded to have children. Twelve children were born; two died at birth. Ten survived. He had nothing. How he got hold of this, I do not know, but the first time he heard me speak in New York City was a Sunday morning, and when we went back to the apartment, he said, "You know, everything you said this morning is true. But why do you tell the people to close their eyes? Don't close your eyes. Keep them partly shut. You can control your imagination and you can control your attention better if the eyes are not completely closed. When you see me in the morning after breakfast reclining in my chair, you might think that I am just sleeping it off – because he's a heavy drinker. "You might think I'm simply sleeping it off. I am not sleeping off anything. I am doing my day's work then! I bring before my mind's eye the men that I want to deal with that day, and I control the conversation. I tell them exactly what I want to tell them, as though it were true. I let them tell me – confirm that it is true, and then when I am completely satisfied with my inner conversation, then I go to town. And it works that way."

Now, he started behind the 8-ball. He had himself, my mother, my grandmother, and the ten of us to feed, plus a few servants. It was not easy. But when he died in 1959, he could leave his ten children – because my mother preceded him by many years, and he never remarried. She died in '41, and he said, "No, I've been so blissfully happy with your Mother, I could not ever get married again," so he remained single until he died at the age of 85. But when he died, that poor man could leave a family of ten independently wealthy – each, not just collectively. He gave it to each individually as a block of stock in the company, just to the ten of us. In 1951 it was then equal to an independent income for each of us. It has tripled since he gave it to us when he died in 1959, under the control of my brother Victor, who practices the same thing.

Victor doesn't smoke and he doesn't drink, but he sits alone, and in his room he, too, is carrying on his little inner conversations – premises of desires fulfilled. And he can completely control that imagination of his. He can completely control the inner conversation, and things work just as he has determined them. He never goes to church. He's a religious man in the true sense of the word. He gives generously to charity and to all people – you would never know how many people he helps in the Island because he doesn't publicize it. That works for him because he has found out inner conversations will do it."...

I spoke of two men tonight: my father and my brother, and they do it by inner conversations. But the Bible supports it. If the Bible did not support it, I wouldn't tell you, but the Bible supports what they are doing. How they found it, I do not know. My father – the only book he ever read was the Bible. I wonder if he got it when he read it?"

In the July 16, 1969 lecture *Many Mansions* Neville said, "I had a mother who understood this law beautifully. Mother wanted to come to this country on a vacation, and she would appropriate it. She would actually...in those days you didn't buy dresses. You brought your dressmaker home and you selected the cloth and she would make you dresses. She had all her dresses made. My father was busy in the business world. He knew nothing of this daily activity of my mother – having all these dresses made. And she appropriated the trip to New York City while physically she was in the little island of Barbados. Then my father would come home and say: "You know – I don't want you here. You don't look very well. You look tired, and so I've just booked you for New York City, and you are sailing next week. All you have to do now is go and get a visa, because you are sailing next week and you are going to be there three months." She would protest: "Oh," she said, "No, Joseph, that's so expensive. You shouldn't do it." Well, she already did it! She knew exactly what she was doing, but he wanted that feeling of one who was being generous, and she knew that he was the man of the house and if he did all these lovely things for her it would be nicer – it would make him feel that he was so generous. And so she pleased him by protesting, when in her heart of hearts she knew exactly what she was doing.

So I say: Do it all in your wonderful Imagination. She would not have done it, if for one moment she thought he couldn't afford it, because she loved him and she loved the children she bore him. But why deprive him of the ability to do it or the desire to do it? Allow him full freedom to have the money to pay for it and the desire to do it. He could have had much more and not have the desire to do it. But she didn't argue with him. She simply appropriated the trip and "lived" in New York City. And as she did it, he had the brilliant idea to send her to New York City. And you wonder: How did it happen? It couldn't happen unless someone moved in Imagination. Whatever takes place is but movement within God, and God is your Imagination! So you can move from one state to another in the twinkling of an eye. You don't need to sit down and burst a blood vessel; you simply do it in the twinkling of an eye. And if you do it with acceptance – with complete acceptance, no doubt as to your Imagination's ability to externalize it – it will externalize it. As we told you last night, the definition of faith is simply the subjective appropriation of the objective hope. You appropriate it subjectively and then it becomes the objective fact."

In 1919 his father believed that there would be a second world war. On June 21, 1971 in the lecture *Secret Of Imagination* Neville said, "I can see my father now, back in 1919. There were ten of us: nine boys and a girl. He was a ship chandler. He had a grocery store, a liquor store and a meat store – a regular little grocery, and he supplied ships, and the ships were bringing the boys back from the First World War, and they would tell him all kinds of stories.

At dinner he would say to my mother, "We will have another war in twenty years. In twenty years there will be another war. It is Germany, but this time, it's going to be Germany and Japan." He didn't mention Italy, but it will be Germany and Japan. "We will then have America as our ally. France will be our ally."

Mother would say, "Joseph, we have nine sons. In twenty years they all will be eligible to go to war." We were all kids in 1919. I was 14 years old.

In 1939, on the 1st day of September war broke – exactly twenty years. What did my father know of any prophecy concerning this? He was only repeating what he had heard from the captains and the stewards and the chief officers as he did business with them. But they were his words! And he said it with conviction, because he believed these men knew what they were talking about."

A friend of Neville asked him about his fathers prediction of the second world war and she told Neville about her father and his attitude toward the friend's brother-in-law. On November 10, 1959 in the lecture *The Only Christianity* Neville said, "Today a friend called me concerning a personal problem. She said, "You said your father has objective vision. He could see the images of his imagining as real as the forms of Nature." I knew this is true. The whole vast world that he built for his ten children, he built out of his wonderful imagination. He would sit alone and conjure before him men and women and see situations as he wanted to see them. And then he would arrest that state just before sleep and he controlled it completely. And when he later returned to his offices and these things came to pass, he was not surprised. Others set the deals in motion that he had already seen in his mind's eye.

This lady called to tell me about her sister's husband. Her father had opposed the marriage and had said that this man would never be any good, and he had set forth in detail just what he would do. He said, "He will father your child but he will not support it. He will live in a bar and he will always be worthless." This man has fulfilled that prophecy in every detail. Her father was a powerful figure in the theater and disliked his son-in-law and prophesied his future and it has come true in detail. I told this lady a story about a prophecy of my father's years ago.

In 1919 at the turn of the year, I can see my father at the head of the table and all of us children sitting there and he said to my mother, "There will be a war in 20 years, Wilsey. It will be in the fall. Germany will again be at war with England. Japan will be in it, and Russia and Italy. America will be our great ally." My mother looked around the table at her sons and said, "My boys will be of the age to go to that war. What are you talking about?" He said, "It will be true and already all the ships are discussing it." He was a ship's chandler and talked with many people. My father did not know that this power he had of imagining as God.

He could take a man or woman or a community and see them so vividly in imagining in his own living room that they became objective to him, and afterwards find them coming to his office to propose what he had inwardly set in motion. But he did not identify that power that creates his world with this supreme power that he called God. "Ever since the creation of the world his invisible nature, his eternal power, has been clearly perceived in the things that have been made."

My father saw everything as made. He discussed a program with a man and afterward the man comes to him and proposes the deal that my father had already closed in his Imagination. But he did not identify it with God. "They exchanged the glory of the immortal God for images resembling mortal man . . . and served the creature rather than the Creator."

Everyone here – your invisible presence is God, but if you imagine money into being and you make a million, suddenly you worship the million, not the power that made it possible. You enter a certain social circle and then you forget that you brought it into being by imagining and now you think this group is what is all-important. So man forgets and exchanges the glory of the immortal God for the image of a mortal man or something that vanishes. For everything visible will vanish; but you will not vanish. Even this great land will one day be washed by the sea but you will not be. That which brought things into being cannot cease to be. So we are warned.

I told this lady about my father and she said, "Your father did that in 1919, but I will go back to 1919, and my father said, 'I do not want to buy a paper because I can see the headlines and they say WAR!' He was so determined and convinced that he would not buy one for weeks, and when he did finally buy it, the headline said, WAR!" Then the lady asked if her father's attitude towards the sister's husband had determined what happened, and whether she should continue helping her sister who was always in need. Yes, it determined what happened. But now it could be changed radically. Give to the sister if she needs help. But then I told her that this power is all imagining and it is one issue with our own wonderful Imagination. There is only ONE. We do not differ in nature or substance from IT but only in degree of intensity. If we could imagine anything in the world and not swerve and not turn and give all glory to this power called God, nothing could keep it from coming into being....

This lady can change the picture for her sister's husband. She can imagine that he is now generous, because now he has so much that he wants to give to her as she gave to him, and she can break the spell cast on him. I know my mother when she darned our socks [she] dreamed for each of us of a future of which she would be proud. Everyone of us is living a noble life and I know she dreamed it for all of us. She never spared her shoe, wham! If you did something wrong. She left the world with her dream fixed in her mind and it came true. We can dream for ourselves or for our neighbors and that dream is the voice of God, for God speaks to man through the medium of a dream"

On December 2, 1968 in the lecture *God's Almighty Power* Neville talks about his father. Neville said, "Many years ago my father and brother, Victor, went to see a spot overlooking the water on 35 acres, which is quite large on the island of Barbados. Three sisters lived in a home there, and sold their cattle to my father. At the time he mentioned he would be interested in purchasing their property if they should ever desire to sell. Then, turning to Victor, he said: "This would be the ideal spot for a hotel." A few years later the ladies decided to sell. One man with a great deal of money wanted those 35 acres very much, but was in Brazil the day my father - who had imagined owning it - bought it. Now a beautiful hotel is on that spot. It is very popular and always crowded, winter and summer, all because my father had a dream and dared to trust the Lord his God, who he knew to be within himself.

My father would never go to church. He didn't like the minister at all. What wonderful stories we have of my father and the minister. One day the minister said to my father: "I am one of the chosen." My father looked at him and said: "I wouldn't have chosen you." He was just as brash as that with everything he did. He had no respect for the man. He never saw the inside of a church, except when we children were baptized. When my sixth brother was to be baptized - by this same minister - my father took two sea captains as godfathers. At the last moment the minister asked if the two gentlemen were Episcopalians, and when one claimed to be a Presbyterian and the other a Methodist, the minister informed my father that the child could not be baptized with these men as godfathers. With that my father said: "Give me my son. I will baptize him myself." He took the child out of the minister's arms, dipped his free hand in the water, sprinkled it on the child's face and said: "In the name of Jesus, your name is Fred" and walked out. And that's his name -Fred Goddard. That's the kind of man my father was and still is. Not a bone in his body lacked courage. He found the Lord as his own wonderful human imagination, so when he wanted something he simply imagined he had it, and walked in that knowledge."

Victor Goddard

Edward Victor Goddard (6/2/1902 - 10/5/1977) was Neville's second oldest brother. On October 13, 1921 Victor and his father Joseph formed a partnership and opened a meat and grocery store located on a side street in Bridgetown, Barbados. On October 13, 1924, exactly three years later, the building that Victor imagined was owned by the Goddard family was purchased. On July 19, 1968 in the lecture *Live In The End* Neville said, "You imagine yourself having a marvelous business, and then comes the day a building is for sale and you haven't a nickel towards it, and a total – not a total stranger, but a man comes in and asks you quite in a friendly manner, "Are you going to buy it?" And knowing you don't have a penny, you say to him, as would a friend to a friend, "With what?" And then he says, "Well, I have money. It's only in the bank drawing nothing." You say, "Well, I have no collateral." But he says, "I've watched you. You are an honest person, your family – they are honest – I think they are. Would you like me to buy it for you and get my lawyer to bid for it? If they knew that I am bidding, they know that I have money, they will bid me up, and so I'll get it at the very lowest price by getting a lawyer who represents more than one client, and they do not know whom he represents, and he'll bid for it. Are you willing to take it, regardless of the price?" and you say, "Yes, I'll take it, but I have no collateral."

"All I need is your signature that you will simply pay six percent of whatever the price is, and then reduce that principal over a period of ten years. Agreed?"

"Yes."

"Well, then, sign this, and we'll see if we can buy it."

That day you own the building, and you don't have one nickel when you own the building that day! You only had your signature on a piece of paper. At the end of 10 years you repay the man his principal; you reduce it every year, pay him six percent on the remaining principal, and reduce the entire thing at the end of ten years.

The man died twenty years later and leaves you $150,000 in cash, tax free, and a couple of homes, many personal belongings. In the meanwhile, you continue in that business, and it multiplies and multiplies, and that year was 1922 – and 1924. This is now 1968. That building – I'm speaking factually – that building in 1924 is now gone. He paid only $50,000 for it. It was repaid and repaid. A bank – three years ago bought the property – the building was rotted – bought the property for $840,000 in cash, and no capital gain – from $50,000 to $840,000. Meanwhile, the business has expanded into all the other islands, so that today you couldn't buy them for $15,000,000. All in imagination! And this goes back to the imagination that preceded this man's offer to buy the building; for the young man, seeing this building and entertaining the thought that the present owners deceived his father, and through deception got him out of a partnership – a junior partnership. And he was moved – not to get even, but to prove that he really had something within him and could be a success in spite of this deception.

So, every day he would see on that marquee, not their name, but his own family's name, and he would see it in his mind's eye, because you could not take their name and transliterate it and make it spell this man's family's name, but he saw it. In his mind's eye he saw that name, which if true would imply the family owned it. He did it every day, twice a day, for two years, and then came this sudden – out of the nowhere, and the whole thing was made possible, and today they are all over the islands, and they have no partners. They have never taken in one partner, never sold one bit of stock outside of the family ownership. All by imagination!

Now, I know what I'm talking about because I'm a member of that family. I am speaking of my own family. This is not hearsay. I know it. My second brother, Victor, in whose imagination this whole thing began to bloom – and he still works all by imagination, he knows what he wants – and then, after having decided in himself, "That's what I want, and that's good for the business, he then, in his mind's eye, appropriates it, and then lets things happen....

So, if I assume that I am, I don't have to have evidence to support it – I assume that I am. Am what? Well, I name it, and having given it a name – given it form, given it definition – remaining in it, I resurrect it. And if it takes a thousand men to aid the birth of that state, a thousand men will play their parts, and I don't have to go out and look for them, any more than my brother had to go out and look for this man. He would not have known where to start looking for one the day of the sale. So far as he is concerned, he had done it in his mind's eye, and he allowed everything to happen, and he comes right in like a joke. He really thought it was a joke, and he said to this man, "Are you fooling me?"

He said, "No."

He said, "Well, then, wait. Let me call my father. He's at lunch." He called him on the wire. He said, "Daddy, come on up. Leave everything and come." And then he said, "Now, you tell my father what you told me."

My father's name is Joseph, and my father said, "You really mean it?"

He said, "Yes, Joe, I mean it. I'll have him bid today. You put your signature here and your son Victor put his signature – that's all I need."

That was a lifetime friendship. So, when that man died, he didn't owe my brother Victor anything. He so loved the friendship and the feeling of – well, decency, that he had with my brother Victor, he gave him $150,000 in cash, and that was tax free, and the homes – everything was tax free. And that building which he bought for $50,000 was sold three years ago to the Bank of Nova Scotia. They tore it down and built a lovely structure, but they paid our family $840,000 for that building, and there was no capital gains tax. The whole thing was simply free."

In the lecture *Order Your Conversations Aright* Neville adds, "I know in my father's case, he was a living example. My Brother Victor is a living example of this technique, but I don't think my father taught it to him. He really got it innately, because he told me that when he saw the sign on a building that had the name "P. N. Roach and Company", he made it spell "J. N. Goddard & Sons." When he confided to my Mother, my Mother said, "Vic, don't do it. We have no money, and it's only going to hurt you. You can never own that building." Two years later the building was up for sale; the business that was in it failed.

A total stranger came in. When I say, "total stranger" – he knew us only as a family, but he had never come to our home for a cup of tea. We were never entertained in his home for a cup of tea, and he was not a drinking partner of my father. He knew him. The day it went up for sale, he came in and said that he would buy it for us. All he would take as collateral was our signature, for we had invested in it our honesty and the bank assured him that if we pledged ourselves, we would do it. If we had to starve to pay his note, we would do it.

He said, "That's all I need, so if you will sign this piece of paper, I'll buy the building. I will have my lawyer bid for it. If I bid for it, they will bid me up, but if my lawyer bids for it, he represents more than one client, and they do not know who he represents today. They wouldn't think for one second that a planter – he was a planter – that he would bid for a business on Main Street which carries groceries."

So, that day the Goddards owned it, and all we had to give was our signature on that paper that we signed. And he said to reduce the principle in ten years, and as you reduce it, you simply pay 6 percent on the principle; if you keep on reducing it every year, in ten years it must be completely paid off. Well, it was. And when he died, twenty years later, he said his greatest friend was Victor Goddard, and he left him an estate in excess of a quarter of a million, tax-free. Everything was completely paid off when he gave that to my Brother Victor. He said, 'You have been my friend.'"

Neville talks about Victor in the lecture *If You Can Really Believe* on June 15, 1970. He said, "My father found it. My brother Victor found it, and then he shared it with the family; and today, here in the little island they are having all the disturbances that we have here.

To us, it's a big scale because the island is small, and here we are two hundred-odd million people. We balloon things here. We make one crisis after the other. Why, I do not know, but we do it – to sell papers and to do all kinds of things. But when you are on a little island and they burn buildings and destroy property, and burn cane – which is destroying the yearly supply, and yet, in spite of it all, one holding a vision that it never fails, and he pays higher and higher and higher dividends. I speak from experience because I am one of the recipients of those dividends. He doesn't care what they are doing. He remains faithful to his vision.

His vision was that "I will be the biggest" – and when I say I, he meant the family would be, but he was the spokesman for the family – he had the vision – "in the entire area. Let them do what they will, I will be the biggest, the most powerful financial giant in the island." Well, he is 68 now, he may depart tonight – I do not know, but his dream has come true…

But you can't wish it, and then deviate and turn away. You must want to be, and so want to be it that you don't turn to anything else.

So, when I go home and I talk to him, he says, "Neville – all right, thank you for your visions. You have visions, and I have another goal. My goal, as you call it, is the world of Caesar. I want the world of Caesar; and so when I depart this world, I am quite willing to have anyone who is in control give me another job, to go on and do it and succeed in the doing. But while I am here, I am going to do what you call 'the things of Caesar.' You do what you call 'the works of God.' I love you as my brother, and you can continue in your visions. But while I am here, I want to be, and I will be" – and by the Law today he is, beyond all doubts and no one would question his position in the financial world in the Island of Barbados. And it doesn't stop there; it goes into the other islands.

So he says, "Let them riot, let them burn, let them do what they want. I will not falter in my vision. And my vision, as I had it for myself when we had nothing – and I got tired of having nothing and having the family looked down upon," so now they don't look down upon them. They all come to them, including the government, and ask them what to do, because they have the know-how, because they have proven it – what to do."

Neville describes the conversation he had with Victor in the lecture *I Remember When* on April 10, 1968. He said, "A few years ago while in Barbados I asked my brother about the business and he replied quite innocently: "It is doing remarkably well. The man who owns two-thirds of it is a good manager, but his hours are long and I think he is getting tired." Six months ago the man asked my brother to buy him out, stating that the hours were too long and the responsibility too great. My brother set that whole thing in motion, and because the man wanted out, my brother got the business at his price. Victor has done this many times before, but not from revelation unless my father told him.

One day the two of them were standing on fifty acres of undeveloped land, which opened to the beach, when my father said: "You know Vic, this would be a good place to build homes and hotels." The property was then owned by three sisters who were not interested in selling, but one day when they were ready to sell, the man who had really wanted the property was in Brazil so my father bought it."

You Are In Barbados!

In the lecture *Thinking Fourth-Dimensionally lesson 3* Neville tells the story about his desire to go to Barbados and of his friend Abdullah. He said, "Let me tell you why I am doing what I am doing today. It was back in 1933 in the city of New York, and my old friend Abdullah, with whom I studied Hebrew for five years, was really the beginning of the eating of all my superstitions. When I went to him I was filled with superstitions. I could not eat meat, I could not eat fish, I could not eat chicken, I could not eat any of these things that were living in the world. I did not drink, I did not smoke, and I was making a tremendous effort to live a celibate life.

Abdullah said to me, "I am not going to tell you 'you are crazy' Neville, but you are you know. All these things are stupid." But I could not believe they were stupid.

In November, 1933, I bade goodbye to my parents in the city of New York as they sailed for Barbados. I had been in this country 12 years with no desire to see Barbados. I was not successful and I was ashamed to go home to successful members of my family. After 12 years in America I was a failure in my own eyes. I was in the theater and made money one year and spent it the next month. I was not what I would call by their standards nor by mine a successful person.

Mind you when I said goodbye to my parents in November I had no desire to go to Barbados. The ship pulled out, and as I came up the street, something possessed me with a desire to go to Barbados.

It was the year 1933, I was unemployed and had no place to go except a little room on 75th Street. I went straight to my old friend Abdullah and said to him "Ab, the strangest feeling is possessing me. For the first time in 12 years I want to go to Barbados."

"If you want to go Neville, you have gone," he replied.

That was very strange language to me. I am in New York City on 72nd Street and he tells me I have gone to Barbados. I said to him, "What do you mean, I have gone, Abdullah?"

He said, "Do you really want to go?"

I answered "yes."

He then said to me, "As you walk through this door now you are not walking on 72nd Street, you are walking on palm lined streets, coconut lined streets; this is Barbados. Do not ask me how you are going to go. You are in Barbados. You do not say 'how' when you 'are there'. You are there. Now you walk as though you were there."

I went out of his place in a daze. I am in Barbados. I have no money, I have no job, I am not even well clothed, and yet I am in Barbados.

He was not the kind of a person with whom you would argue, not Abdullah. Two weeks later I was no nearer my goal than on the day I first told him I wanted to go to Barbados. I said to him, "Ab, I trust you implicitly but here is one time I cannot see how it is going to work. I have not one penny towards my journey, I began to explain."

You know what he did. He was as black as the ace of spades, my old friend Abdullah, with his turbaned head. As I sat in his living room he rose from his chair and went towards his study and slammed the door, which was not an invitation to follow him. As he went through the door he said to me, "I have said all that I have to say."

On the 3rd of December I stood before Abdullah and told him again I was no nearer my trip. He repeated his statement, "You are in Barbados."

The very last ship sailing for Barbados that would take me there for the reason I wanted to go, which was to be there for Christmas, sailed at noon on December 6th, the old Nerissa.

On the morning of December 4th, having no job, having no place to go, I slept late. When I got up there was an airmail letter from Barbados under my door. As I opened the letter a little piece of paper flickered to the floor. I picked it up and it was a draft for $50.00.

The letter was from my brother Victor and it read, "I am not asking you to come, Neville, this is a command. We have never had a Christmas when all the members of our family were present at the same time. This Christmas it could be done if you would come."

My oldest brother Cecil left home before the youngest was born and then we started to move away from home at different times so never in the history of our family were we ever all together at the same time.

The letter continued, "You are not working, I know there is no reason why you cannot come, so you must be here before Christmas. The enclosed $50.00 is to buy a few shirts or a pair of shoes you may need for the trip. You will not need tips; use the bar if you are drinking. I will meet the ship and pay all your tips and your incurred expenses. I have cabled Furness, Withy & Co. in New York City and told them to issue you a ticket when you appear at their office. The $50.00 is simply to buy some little essentials. You may sign as you want aboard the ship. I will meet it and take care of all obligations."

I went down to Furness, Withy & Co. with my letter and let them read it. They said, "We received the cable Mr. Goddard, but unfortunately we have not any space left on the December 6th sailing. The only thing available is 3rd Class between New York and St. Thomas. When we get to St. Thomas we have a few passengers who are getting off. You may then ride 1st Class from St. Thomas to Barbados. But between New York and St. Thomas you must go 3rd Class, although you may have the privileges of the 1st Class dining room and walk the decks of the 1st Class."

I said, "I will take it."

I went back to my friend Abdullah on the afternoon of December 4th and said, "It worked like a dream." I told him what I had done, thinking he would be happy. Do you know what he said to me? He said, "Who told you that you are going 3rd Class? Did I see you in Barbados, the man you are, going 3rd Class? You are in Barbados and you went there 1st Class."

I did not have one moment to see him again before I sailed on the noon of December 6th. When I reached the dock with my passport and my papers to get aboard that ship the agent said to me, "We have good news for you, Mr. Goddard. There has been a cancellation and you are going 1st Class."

Abdullah taught me the importance of remaining faithful to an idea and not compromising. I wavered, but he remained faithful to the assumption that I was in Barbados and had traveled 1st Class...

Feast on the idea, become identified with the idea as though you were already that embodied state. Walk in the assumption that you are what you want to be. If you feast on that and remain faithful to that mental diet, you will crystallize it. You will become it in this world.

When I came back to New York in 1934, after three heavenly months in Barbados, I drank, I smoked, and did everything I had not done in years.

I remembered what Abdullah had said to me, "After you have proven this law you will become normal, Neville. You will come out of that graveyard, you will come out of that dead past where you think you are being holy. For all you are really doing you know, you are being so good, Neville, you are good for nothing"

I came back walking this earth a completely transformed person. From that day, which was in February 1934, I began to live more and more. I cannot honestly tell you I have always succeeded. My many mistakes in this world, my many failures would convict me if I told you that I have so completely mastered the movements of my attention that I can at all times remain faithful to the idea I want to embody.

But I can say with the ancient teacher, although I seem to have failed in the past, I move on and strive day after day to become that which I want to embody in this world. Suspend judgment, refuse to accept what reason and the senses now dictate, and if you remain faithful to the new diet, you will become the embodiment of the ideal to which you remain faithful.

If there is one place in the world that is unlike my little island of Barbados, it is New York City. In Barbados the tallest building is three stories, and the streets are lined with palm trees and coconut trees and all sorts of tropical things. In New York City you must go to a park to find a tree.

Yet I had to walk the streets of New York as though I walked the streets of Barbados. To one's imagination all things are possible. I walked, feeling that I was actually walking the streets of Barbados, and in that assumption I could almost smell the odor of the cocoanut lined lanes. I began to create within my mind's eye the atmosphere I would physically encounter were I in Barbados.

As I remained faithful to this assumption, somebody canceled passage and I received it. My brother in Barbados, who never thought of my coming home, has the commanding urge to write me a strange letter. He had never dictated to me, but this time he dictated, and thought that he originated the idea of my visit.

I went home and had three heavenly months, returned 1st Class, and brought back quite a sum of cash in my pocket, a gift. My trip, had I paid for it, would have been $3,000, yet I did it without a nickel in my pocket.

"I have ways ye know not of. My ways are past finding out." The dimensionally greater self took my assumption as the command and influenced the behavior of my brother to write that letter, influenced the behavior of someone to cancel that 1st Class passage, and did all the things necessary that would tend toward the production of the idea with which I was identified.

I was identified with the feeling of being there. I slept as though I were there, and the entire behavior of man was molded in harmony with my assumption. I did not need to go down to Furness, Withy & Co. and beg them for a passage, asking them to cancel someone who was booked 1st Class. I did not need to write my brother and beg him to send me some money or buy me a passage. He thought he originated the act. Actually, to this day, he believes that he initiated the desire to bring me home.

My old friend Abdullah simply said to me, 'You are in Barbados, Neville. You want to be there; wherever you want to be, there you are. Live as though you are and that you shall be.'"

On June 9, 1969 in the lecture *The First Principle* Neville shared a little more detail on how he imagined the trip to Barbados. He said, "I wanted a trip I could not afford, yet I traveled over 5,000 miles by being still and saying to myself: "My awareness is God and all things are possible to him. therefore what I am imagining will come to pass." Then I began to imagine I was on a ship sailing towards Barbados. I remained faithful to that act, when suddenly - after twelve years - I received a letter from the family saying they would take care of all of my expenses if I would come home for Christmas. So I proved it. Then I tried it again and again, and the more I tried it the more I realized that the statement in the 46th Psalm was true: that God really is my own wonderful consciousness, for I learned to be still and know that I am God."

Neville wondered whether he should control people using his imagination. In the lecture *Esau And Jacob* on November 13, 1959 Neville said, "When I wanted to go to Barbados and did not have a penny, I slept in my Imagination in Barbados and saw the world from Barbados, and I went there through the efforts of my family, who thought they had initiated the trip. When I identified myself with a state, others responded. They moved like automatons. And then I wondered if I should do it, and then I went back to that passage in Genesis: "You shall serve your brother." And every man in the world you shall serve. And then you feel right about it. This one was imagining and every being in the world is serving him. You do not have to ask anyone in the world to help you, no matter what 'they' say."

In 1945 Neville and his family went to Barbados on a one way ticket and had to be back by the first week of May for a commitment in Milwaukee. In the 1971 lecture *Imagination Plus Faith* Neville said, "Years ago, right after the Second World War – the year was 1945, I sailed with my little family, my wife and daughter out to the Island of Barbados. I hadn't seen the family through the war years, because there was no transportation available. I was in the Army for a very short span of time, about four months. Because of my age plus this law, I was honorably discharged because I was over 38. My son was in the Marines in Guadalcanal, but my little girl was only a matter of months in age. So, at the end of 1945 I sailed, on the first ship out, for there were no planes taking any one to the Indies. So, I sailed with my wife and my little girl on a one-way ticket, not thinking for one moment of the difficulty in getting back to New York, and I had a commitment to be in Milwaukee in the first week of May. So, I sailed [at] the end of December – New Year's Eve, to be exact. At the end of about three months, my brother Victor said to me, "You have a return ticket?" and I said, "No, but I want to get back the first week of May to go to Milwaukee." He said, "How dare you leave the capital of the financial world, New York City, without making arrangements? All things are done there, and you have come to a little island like Barbados, and we have two little ships – one carrying a maximum of 65 passengers, and the other carrying a maximum of 120, one sailing out of Boston, one sailing out of New York, but all these islands are to be serviced, and we alone could use more ships several times a month. They only make a round trip – one makes it every 21 days, and the other one makes it every 32 days; and how dare you come out, knowing you must be back, without making any arrangement in New York City?"

Well, it was perfectly all right. I sat in my hotel room in a nice big easy chair, and I assumed it was a little boat that would tend the ship because we didn't have a deep harbor in those days. We have one now, but there was no deep-water harbor, so I assumed that I was on a small little boat taking me out to the ship, and that my brother Victor and sister Daphne, my wife and other members of the family and little Vicki were all aboard the boat. Then I assumed that I was stepping off this little boat onto the gangplank. I could feel the rhythm; I could feel it give as I went up step after step after step. My mind wandered before I got to the top. So, I came back to the bottom again and started all over. It wandered again; I came back to the bottom and did it over.

When I got to the top I had no room where I could go. I simply assumed now: My hand is on the rail. I could feel the salt of the sea on the rail. I could feel the salt of the sea in the air, and then I looked towards the Island of Barbados with a mixed feeling: one of sadness because I was leaving the family, and one of joy because I was going back to America where I live. That was a peculiar feeling, but it was a natural feeling. And while I had hold of the rail and assumed this state, I then fell asleep in the chair.

Now, I must go back. When I went down to the firm in Barbados to ask for transportation, they said, "You haven't the chance of a snowball in hell of getting out of Barbados until October." This was then the month of late March. Not a chance of getting out! They had a list that long and I was at the bottom of the list. Trinidad had a list that much longer, for they had so many more people. All the islands have lists. There were literally thousands of people waiting to get aboard, and they only had two ships, one carrying 65 and one carrying 120 passengers. So, they said, "Mr. Goddard, you have no chance of getting out before October." I said, "All right."

Then I sat and did that which would imply that I was sailing. I simply did exactly what I knew I had to do. I simply subjectively appropriated my objective hope. I hoped to be sailing on that ship, and so I subjectively appropriated the objective hope, for if I were sailing I would get into that little boat, get off onto the gangplank and walk up to the deck of the ship. The next day – the very next day – I had not dressed; I had not a thing to do but go to the bathing beach later on in the day. The phone rang, and it was the Alcoa Steamship Company asking me to come on down, that they had news for me. I asked them what news. They said we have passage for three sailing on the next ship, which will put you back in New York City on the 1st of May.

I went down, and I was very curious and asked, "Why do you offer it to me when the list, you told me, is so long, with hundreds and hundreds waiting on it who are all ahead of me? And what caused you to have the vacancy?"

Well, a lady in the island, so she told me, who desired to get out badly and wanted to go back to America – the first choice would be this lady. Well, suddenly she changed her feeling about it. Then they went down the entire list with no reason whatsoever and gave it to us, and they justified it in this manner:

"The ship only carries two in each room, but your little girl is only about three years of age, and she can sleep in a bunk with your wife, and you can have the other one. So, because she is such a little child – only three years old, we gave it to accommodate three rather than two, and the two that we do have couldn't share it anyway because they are different sexes and not married."

That is how she justified giving it to me when hundreds of people were before me. I know how I did it. Every natural effect has a spiritual cause, and not a natural. A natural cause only seems. It is a delusion. Well, I remembered what I did. It was only a matter of 24 hours between planting that seed and the springing of that seed into objective reality. By the 20th day of April I was on that boat, getting off in New York City by May the 1st to meet my appointment in Milwaukee...

Now, take faith, as defined for us in the 11th chapter of the book of Hebrews, and you will see that it is simply the subjective appropriation of the objective hope. I wanted to be on that ship; that was my objective hope. Well, I first subjectively appropriated it. I did it as though it were true. I actually acted just as though the thing had happened. I walked up the gangplank, held the rail, looked back with mixed feelings, and then fell asleep. And when I found myself wandering, I went back to the very first step on the gangplank and did it over again, and went on doing it over and over until I could walk right up that gangplank and actually feel I am at the very top and turn around and put my hand on the rail. And strangely enough, in my imagination I allowed my brother Victor to carry my daughter Victoria up the gangplank, and to justify his action when we got off the little tender onto the gangplank, he said, "Come, your father's arms aren't strong enough to take you. I will take you." But my arms certainly were strong enough to carry my daughter, but he had to justify it, as we all do. He had to justify that action, and then took her up. Well, that is exactly what he did when we got to the little boat!"

Neville shared an experience of him imagining himself in Barbados to make him feel better because about fourteen inches of snow and a low turnout to a lecture. In the lecture *The Potter's House* he said, "I will tell you of an experience of mine. Back in 1941, it was the month of February, and I had come out with the book called "Your Faith Is Your Fortune." My audience in those days in New York City numbered, say, a thousand people three times a week. I thought I would have a fair audience, but that night it snowed and snowed. It started about noon, and kept on snowing. I began my lectures in those days around quarter of nine, and suddenly no one came. I had not more than a hundred people, when I was accustomed to a thousand people. They couldn't get through. We must have had between fourteen and sixteen inches of snow, and no one could get through. So, when I went home I was a little bit disappointed in the attendance because I brought my new book out, and I wanted to have at least a good-sized audience.

That night, this is what I did. In an idle moment – I didn't intend it consciously, but I did it; I went to sleep in my bedroom, and I assumed that I was in Barbados, two thousand miles away across the water to the little island called Barbados. I dropped off to sleep feeling I was in my mother's home. I could hear the coconut leaves against the woodwork.

I could smell the odor that comes only from the tropics. I could feel the entire atmosphere of Barbados, and I thought of New York City and saw it to the north of me, two thousand miles away, and I fell sound asleep in that assumption.

When I woke in the morning, the snow was still on the ground, say, fourteen or fifteen inches of snow. I made plans for my wife and myself to go to Maine in the month of August for a vacation and sent off a deposit to hold my place for me. In the month of August – late August – I got a cable from Barbados saying that Mother was desperately ill, and they didn't want to tell me anything about it because war was on. At least, England was at war. And there was no transportation, just a couple of ships moving out, and they did not want to disturb me. Mother was desperately ill, and it was terminal. There was no possibility of any recovery. And if it was at all possible to make the trip, she wanted to see me before she died. All the others were present. I was the only one who was missing.

In twenty-four hours my wife and I sailed for Barbados. The ship was leaving that night, and we couldn't have gotten together all the things necessary, but we sailed for Barbados instead of going to Maine. I had no plans to go to Barbados, but here suddenly came the cable revealing the need to go to Barbados, and we went to Barbados, and we did not go to Maine.

What I did in February took approximately seven months to mature. I did it – consciously did it, not thinking for one moment – I did it only to relax and to put myself into that mood because I was disappointed that the crowd did not come out and get my new book, "Your Faith Is Your Fortune," So, I tell you from experience, don't do it idly, because when you plant something, that is still coming into being. It is going to come into being and disturb your so-called conscious plans. It works that way. So, I do know that when it comes back into this world, it doesn't really matter. I stand here just perfectly simply now and do something in my mind's eye and give it sensory vividness and give it the tones of reality, and then I open my eyes, and this shocks me, because this tells me that what I just did was self-deception. You deceive yourself. It is all in your imagination. But I know now that my imagination is the only reality; that this world is still the world of imagination, and that all the things that I see as an objective fact in my world – they are all "pushed out" because of my imagined acts."

In the February 3, 1969 lecture *Wonder Working Power* Neville added, "I remember one cold winter night in New York City. I was lecturing in a church off Times Square where the usual crowd was in excess of a thousand, but because of the cold and snow there were only about 200 in attendance. My first book had just been released, and that night maybe 50 copies were sold, and since I had run the presses on 5000 I was eager to get the book in distribution.

Because of the storm outside, that night I spoke of the warmth of Barbados: the palm trees and the odors of the tropics. And when I retired, I felt myself in my mother's home in Barbados. I listened to the movement of the leaves and smelled the tropical atmosphere. Then a cable came saying that mother was dying and I should return home. Within 24 hours my wife and I set sail for Barbados. I had put myself there and had to fulfill my imaginal act, even though it was an inconvenient time for me to go; so I do not treat my wonder working power lightly!

When I ask you to adjust yourself to a certain state, I mean for you to feel it is real, for reality is controlled by feeling. The day will come when feeling will modify, or even void, that which you think are the laws of nature and science, and you will discover they are not so at all."

Catherine Goddard

Catherine Goddard (2/7/1907 - 1/1/1975) was Neville's second wife. They were married on February 25, 1942. She was a costume designer for eleven years before she stopped working in 1946. In the lecture *Many Mansions* on July 16, 1969 Neville talks about her attitude toward the head producer. He said, "My wife, back in 1945, when she left the Music Hall (she worked at the Music Hall for eleven years as a costume designer, and the head producer used to treat her unmercifully) ...but I told her one day: "Darling, he couldn't do anything for you unless you allowed it. You actually feel that he is no earthly good. You feel that you are a cultured American lady. You went to Smith College. You were born and raised in a lovely environment. You never heard unkind things in your home. You never saw anything that was cheap. Your mother had lovely taste, beautiful things." The interior was a beautiful, a huge, enormous home, with eight fireplaces, with every floor beautifully furnished, and she was raised in that environment. She went only to private schools, then off to Smith College, and then she worked in the Music Hall. Well, her father was managing director of the Music Hall, so when she went in there, she did not ask any favors because of her father's position, and this man simply lorded it over her. She would say within herself (this she confessed to me): "Oh, you foreigner!" because he came from Russia. And she mentally would remind him that she is an American by birth for at least six or seven generations, and he came from Russia, and is now acting this way. Well, that's wrong. Whether he be a Russian or American, or English, or anything else, we are all one.

Now, stop it, and allow him to praise you for your work. He's always condemning and always criticizing. Walk to work. You only walk five blocks from where you live to the Music Hall. Just imagine that he is not only praising you for your work, but he wants to use all of your designs, and the budget will not allow it, so he goes to your father and asks your father to increase the budget, that he may be allowed to use all the designs. Your father's a businessman, and he's not going to do it. He's going to cater neither to you nor to him, but he has to run that at a profit for the Rockefellers. So, let him do it. But in your Imagination assume that he does!" How long do you think it took for him to actually change his attitude towards her? I'll tell you: twenty-four hours! When she came downstairs with this wonderful collection of designs, he raved about them, and he actually went to her father and begged him to increase the budget, that he may use them all. Her father would not allow it. And from that day on, he changed his attitude toward her radically for the better. Why? Because she changed hers towards him.

Are we not told in Scripture: "We love Him because He first loved us"? (1 John 4:19) You want to be quite fair? Well, start it here. Start it in your own Imagination, and you'll find it responding on the outside, for the outer world only reflects the inner world. Start it there first, or you will never see it in the outer world! So, as she walked the street she simply imagined he walked with her, praising her for the work that she had done. And in twenty-four hours he praised her, and hoped her father would increase the budget, that he could use all of them. And then she retired. And after she retired in 1946, he begged her to come back and do special shows. She went back and I think she did about six special shows for him. Who would have dreamt that he would ever ask her to come back and do one, after the treatment that she received? She has overcome it; completely overcome it. She knows that it is all within her. She doesn't turn to anyone to blame; she knows it's within her. She tries to find out where, in her, she's been carrying on these unlovely conversations, and then – changing the conversations within her – she changes the world in which she lives."

In the lecture *No Other Gods* on July 16, 1968 he added some more details to the story. He said, "My wife, when we were first married, she worked at the Music Hall, and the man who was her boss – a Russian, would keep her after hours. He wouldn't come to work until noon; she came to work at 9:00, and her hours were from 9:00 until 5:00; but he didn't come until 12:00, and he liked to work late at night, and just as she was about to go home, he would call her into his office and say, Billie, I want you to do this, that, and the other,—and delay her dinner by an hour and a half, two hours, or more. And she resented this attitude of this man; so I said to her, "Why, Darling, as long as you are going to act this way towards him, he has to respond in like kind. You know the law; he doesn't. So he makes a fortune, and you don't make a fortune, but you are an artist." She was a designer for the costumes that appeared on the stage of the Music Hall for eleven years. So, I said, "Talk to him as though he had praised you for your work. This morning when you go to work" – we were only five blocks from the Music Hall where we lived on 55th Street – "as you walk down Sixth Avenue, make a mental picture of him walking with you and hear his voice" – it's a distinctive Russian voice – "and have him in his own broken English tell you how thrilled he is with your designs – so much so that he wants to use all of them, but the budget does not allow it; yet he wants to use every one you've brought down. How would you feel if he wanted all of them, and not take just two or three and send you back to your office to bring another four or five; but he wants every one that you have submitted?"

She started doing it. Do you know? It wasn't 24 hours that his attitude changed towards Bill, and remained changed because she changed it. So, we have that in Scripture: "We love Him, because He first loved us" (I John 4:19). Our love of God is response. Well, your love of anyone is response, unless you know what you are doing and you set it up in motion. And, so, if you want someone to respond, you have to start it first. So, she started it with him – Leonidov and to this day – of course, she hasn't worked there in years – but to this day when we go back, if we go to the Music Hall, he is all praise and joy. He could not be nicer and, yet, for eleven years he was, in her eyes, the devil!

Well, this is life. And it's entirely up to us. What are we going to do if I have no other god? The minute she spoke of him as causation, she had another god and he had the power to do what he was doing, and he had no power because the very day she changed it to the real God, he had no power. He could only reflect the activity of her own mind. So if I think, now he can fire me – then, I've given him a power he doesn't really possess because the world is yourself "pushed out." The whole vast world bears witness of the being that you are; for you are God, and God is a protean being. He's playing all the parts – good, bad and indifferent. So, it's entirely up to us what we are doing, that we conjure in our world the different ones that bear witness to what we are doing. They reflect the activity of our mind."

Neville shares a story about his missing luggage with his wife's dresses that couldn't be replaced for $1500. In the July 13, 1970 lecture called *The Identical Harvest* Neville said, "I will give you one that is very personal. When I planted it, I do not know, but I had to have planted it. And I will show you that, even though you plant unlovely things unwittingly, you need not be the victim. You can revise it, and change it, even though you are confronted with a seemingly insoluble problem.

When I left here last year, in the month of July, I checked my two suitcases at the airport. When I arrived in Los Angeles, one was missing. The contents I could not replace for $1500. They were all the lovely dresses that my wife has, and all her dresses are made by a certain couturier in Beverly Hills, and not one is under $195. She has made these dresses over the years for her. They were not new, but I couldn't replace them – any one – under $195 – plus other things in that suitcase. My suits were in another suitcase, perfectly all right. I recorded the loss. They said, "When we find it, if we find it, we will send it right over to you, Mr. Goddard."

After five days and not a word, we called, and they said, "It is lost. We've made every effort, and it cannot be found. Put in a claim and send it off to San Diego, the headquarters for the PSA office." My wife did the legitimate thing in the world of Caesar. She itemized the contents to the best of her ability and what it would take to replace the items in that suitcase.

That morning about 2:00 o'clock I awoke and said, "Now, look here. I teach this principle, and, so, I have brought about a loss in my own world. I will have none of it! I teach Revision. I heard what the man said over the telephone! 'The thing is lost. They cannot find it; we have looked high and low.'"

Then you read in the papers that hundreds of millions of dollars are stolen every year at our airports, depots, and the wharves across the country, and it's an inside job, as it were. So, at 2:00 o'clock in the morning I took in my hands my suitcase. I felt the weight of it; I could feel the weight. I could see in my mind's eye the gray bag with the black leather. I could actually feel it, and I felt it with the sense of relief, for of all the pleasures in the world, relief is the most keenly felt.

When you are expecting someone, and they are late – someone you truly love, and they are late, and it gets later and later and you get anxious, and then you hear the familiar voice; you know the relief that comes. Well, now, that's what you do when you feel that relief. And, then, I dropped it and got up and went into my living room and simply read my Bible.

It was early. We have a lovely apartment, and it was quiet. We have no neighbors. I turned on the lights and read my Bible. The next day: no report. The following day I received a letter postmarked San Francisco, a strange, peculiar hand printing my name: Neville Goddard. The address was correct. When I opened the letter, there was the little note in the same peculiar printing! "Your suitcase is in Box 524, Sorry. The Phantom," and enclosed a key. So, I called the security guards at the Los Angeles airport, and I told them the contents of the letter. I said, "I have the key."

"Well, we'll investigate immediately," which they did. They called back within a matter of five or ten minutes to tell me that there is no such box in Los Angeles. I reminded them that the letter came from San Francisco, so he said, "All right, I'll call you back." He called San Francisco, and the security guards got the local police, and they opened 524, and there was my suitcase. They opened it up in the presence of the policemen, and the whole thing was ransacked – completely ransacked, utterly turned inside out. They sealed it and flew it down, and asked me to come over with my wife, and in the presence of the security guards in L.A. they would open my suitcase in my presence, which they did.

Not a handkerchief was missing! Everything was turned inside out. The man was most apologetic, and he said, "Mr. Goddard, I am awfully sorry. We are sorry for the Company. These things happen. We do not know how they happen, but they happen. May we clean the things for you?"

I said, "No, that is something that my wife and I do every year. We travel for more than two weeks. Everything we wear is dry-cleaned. So, it is a little problem of ours, and we've always done it."

Then he gave me his personal card and said, "The next time you and Mrs. Goddard travel on PSA, you are our guests." I took the card and gave it to my wife, and now we are here and going back as the guests of PSA. But we did not lose one handkerchief – not a thing, but it was a complete mess. What they were looking for, I do not know, but they found nothing there. However, that's done."

Catherine or Bill, as Neville called her, had an older sister named Alice who was married to Sam Smith Jr. Neville talked about him in the April 2, 1968 lecture *Whom Do You Seek?* Neville said, "Now let me tell you a story I recorded in one of my books. The year was 1950 and the man is my brother-in-law. Having graduated from Harvard, he entered the banking business, where he remained for many years. Now, in the banking profession a promotion occurs only when someone dies, is fired, or resigns. Qualified to hold the finest job, he wanted the best for himself, his wife, and their two children. He was a pillar of the Episcopal Church in New York City, sitting on the planning committee, advising them as to the care of their money, yet he knew nothing of the art of prayer or the secret of Christ.

One day he came to the house, and telling me of his financial desires, he asked what he should do. When I asked him if he would like to be in the investment business, he replied: "I want it more than anything in the world." Then I said: "Go to bed tonight knowing you are now investing large sums of money. Do that night after night and the position you desire will be yours."

Shortly after his visit my family sailed to Barbados, where we remained for three months. When we returned, my brother-in-law and sister came for dinner and this is the story Sam told me. Three weeks after our previous visit he attended a meeting on Wall Street. After the meeting was over a man he had known for years came over to him and asked if he would consider leaving the bank and joining him. He then quoted a salary which was twice what Sam was presently making, as well as promising him a five week paid vacation every year. Well, Sam was stunned beyond measure. He went home, discussed the offer with his wife, and they agreed it was a marvelous opportunity. That day he began his investment career representing the Rockefeller brothers - not the foundation, but the five brothers and their sister. He never bought stock, only suggested it. One day he told me he worked with one portfolio for $394 million, and that's just one of many! Sam remained there for eight years, leaving to become a junior partner in a brokerage firm.

I wrote his story in one of my books and gave him a copy. A short time later while visiting them I discovered my book had found its place on a top shelf, completely out of reach. They had read the book, but as a pillar of the church with its orthodox concept of things, they could not associate the Jesus they worshiped with what they did, and the next time I went to their home, my book was completely out of sight. As a Harvard man, he could not believe that one who had never seen the inside of a college had helped him.

So whom do you seek? Is it not Jehovah, the savior of the world? The one who created all things, and without him there is not a thing made that is made? Sam knew what he did to get the job, but he could not believe that what he did was Jesus. Through the years we have remained close and dear friends, but never has one word been said concerning this. At dinner he gives grace and thanks someone on the outside for their food, doing it by rote. He can't help it, for it is part of his training, but the day will come when he will discover who Jesus is. He found him, but - unable to recognize him - he turned his back upon the one and only one [who] is Jesus Christ. We are told: "He who is not with me is against me and he who will not gather with me, scatters." At the present time Sam is not with me, but continues to worship something on the outside. Now you see how practical this story is.

Do you seek Jesus? Say "I am" and you have found him. Man finds it so difficult to understand that his own wonderful human imagination is the being he is seeking, but the day will come when he will find him. On that day Jesus' Son will stand before him and call him "Father". Jesus is not Jehovah's son as you were taught. Jesus is Jehovah. Now, if Jehovah has a son and Jesus is Jehovah, is not David the Son? One day the veil will be lifted and God's Son, David, will stand before you and call you "Father". Until then, although many will listen to my words, they - like my brother-in-law - will not accept it.

Everything came about as Sam desired it to be. They are now living in a beautiful apartment. Their children have graduated from Smith and Harvard and in two more years he plans to retire and travel throughout the world. Sam found Jesus but did not recognize him. He is still looking for something on the outside - but may I tell you: no physical man is Jesus.

If anyone comes to you saying he is a holy man, do not believe him. Jesus is holy, for Jesus is Jehovah, he who can only be recognized through his Son, as it takes God's Son, David, to reveal your true identity, that of being the Lord God Jehovah. Jesus Christ, that's who you really are, and only God's Son can reveal it to you. I know the truth of which I speak, for it has happened to me. The world teaches that everything is on the outside. That your success or failure depends upon where you live, the church you attend, your school or college education. This they believe because they do not know Jesus Christ, who is their own wonderful human imagination!

When I asked Sam, he told me that regardless of how disillusioned or tired he was, he imagined every night, and that although he had known the gentleman for many years, he had never been approached until three weeks after he had applied this principle. Sam saw the results of what he did. He knew he did it, but he could not believe that what he did was Jesus Christ!...

Now, what I have told you this night about my brother-in-law can be applied to transcend any limitation desired, I don't care what it is. I knew by nature Sam would do what he said he would. He had promised that even though it was not rational (and Sam is a rational man), he would sleep in the assumption his desire was fulfilled until I returned from Barbados. Then he would tell me it didn't work! Knowing Sam would not falter in the doing, I knew by that time it would be done, and of course it was. So I urge everyone to take my words seriously and try it. When you go to bed tonight, catch the feeling that would be yours if your desire were now realized. Then fall asleep in that feeling. If you do it, you will not fail. How it is going to happen I do not know; I only know that if you do it, it will happen. And when it does, don't forget the lesson you have learned.

Sam has money now and continues to invest it in the world of Caesar, but has forgotten the principle behind it all and is looking for a physical Jesus on the outside. May I tell you: he has a great surprise in store for him, for when he dies, there will be no Jesus there to welcome him. Instead he will be restored to life in a body the same as before. His body will be young and unbelievably new, as he finds himself in an environment best suited for the work yet to be done in him. This he will continue to do until he finds and believes in Jesus"

Neville talked about his wife feeling that she was married to him before they were really married. In the July 23, 1968 lecture *Power* he said, "The unmarried, if you desire to be married – what symbol in the world would imply that you are married? A little band? In this western world a little band around this ring finger – not around any other finger – around this finger. It doesn't have to be the biggest aspidistra in the world, just a plain little gold ring. If you wore it there, it would imply you're married. Sleep tonight as though you wore one. Don't put your physical thumb on it; put your imaginary thumb on it, and feel it in your imagination. You can do it! Feel a ball. Can you feel it? Then feel a piece of silk. Feel this, one after the other. Can you discriminate between all these different sensations? If you can discriminate between this and a tennis ball and a baseball and a piece of silk, then you can't discriminate between nothings. They must exist. Though unseen by your eyes they still must exist!

So, if I can discriminate between these unseen objects, these objects, though unseen, must be real. Well, now take that and put it there, but feel when you wear it, that you are proud of the one who put it there. You don't have to see what he looks like. When it's put there, you'll be proud of his name, to bear it, and you'll be proud of him. Just put it there.

Do you know why I know that? My wife did it. She did it! Actually, she did it. One day she was in the presence of a so-called sensitive, and this one said to her, "Why did you take off your wedding ring?"

She said, "I am not married."

"Oh," she said, "don't fool me. You took off your wedding ring."

She said, "But I'm not married."

She said, "I'll even tell you his name," and she started off with Neb –Neba – Neva – she didn't quite get it but she was coming very, very close to it. She was actually sensing what my wife in consciousness was feeling.

When I first met her, I wanted her. The very first day I knew her I wanted to marry her, but I was entangled. Was I entangled! But, by this law, I disentangled myself. Without hurting anyone, I disengaged myself from all these complexities so that I could actually legitimately say, "Will you marry me?" But in the meanwhile she was wearing the ring. I hadn't yet put it there, but she allowed me to put it there and slept as though I had put it there.

So I tell you unmarried ladies, if you desire to be married (maybe you don't) – if you do, that's the way to do it. And he'll come out of the nowhere. You don't have to go and buy anyone or try to meet the right people. Usually when you try to meet the right one, he's always the wrong one. So don't go searching. Those who go searching for love only make manifest their own love-less-ness, and the loveless never find love. Only the loving find love, and they never have to seek for it. You draw them; they come to you. "

Neville

As a boy Neville dreamed of coming to America. On January 7, 1969 in the lecture *Your Maker* he said, "When I was a boy I lived in Barbados. Unschooled, with no background whatsoever, I dreamed of coming to America. I became so enamored with the idea, that at the age of 17 my parents put me on a boat to America with $600 in my pocket. They thought I would come back once the money was gone, but I wanted to live in America so badly I had to come and make it my home.

Are you willing to become enamored over a desire that much? Are you willing to fall in love with its fulfillment that you imagine it is yours now? If so, I promise you it will outpicture itself in your world. And when it does, you will have found Christ, for the words of scripture: 'By him all things are made and without him is not anything made that is made,' are false.

When you test your imagination you will find He who produced your desire and the Maker of all things! I have tested him numberless times. I have taught this principle to others who have tested him and shared their experiences with me.

In the lecture *Freedom* on October 28, 1968 Neville said, "One day I was fired from J. C. Penney Co. Working for a year and a half, running their elevator and being their errand boy, making $22. a week and paying $5. room rent, I could not understand it when they let me go. But my dreams, my desires, transcended my position there, so they had to do what they did in order for my desires to be realized. Believe me, you are the cause of the phenomena of your life - be it good, bad or indifferent. If, to you the news is distasteful, you are the dreamer of that distasteful storm. But the day will come when you will awake to discover that the storm is over. That there is only one cause, and that is awareness! I know it is easier to give advice and show the other person where he is wrong, than it is to acknowledge that he is only reflecting the wrong in you. It is difficult to accept the concept that the world is bearing witness to your thoughts, but it is true. If you do not like something or someone, do not look at it or them; look within to the one who is causing the image"

Neville shares a story about getting food poisoning in the June 4, 1971 lecture *Gifts Bestowed By God* Neville said, "And so, until one gets out of a state, don't try to hit him over the head. He can't hear you. He knows what he is doing is the only truth, the only reality. If he really believes that clams are going to poison him, do you know? They'll poison him. You and I will sit down and eat the most glorious bunch of clams; he will sit and eat the same from the same dish and they will poison him. I had that experience when I was a strict vegetarian.

I went to Toronto. A friend of mine invited me – we were house guests. She could ill afford the salmon that she prepared – a beautiful salmon, but I was not eating fish or meat or fowl or anything in those days; but as a guest, I was trained never to offense a host, and so I forced myself to eat what was put before me. That was the first time I broke my fast in these many years. Do you know? There were seven of us at the table: my host and hostess, my dancing partner, her mother, and then two sons – there were a bunch of us around; and I was the only one with Ptomaine Poisoning. I came down – I was poisoned and poisoned beyond measure that night, and every one ate the same fish. But I was eating against the grain of my own being. I knew I was doing wrong by my own – at the moment – my own ethical code, and I was poisoned, and they all survived. Well, my body survived, too; but I mean, I was really sick.

So, the most marvelous thing in the world will poison you if you think that it is wrong in what you do. So, where is it? All in your own wonderful human imagination. That is God!"

Mary Hughes (3/29/1901 - 11/9/1979) was Neville's first wife. They were married on October 18, 1923. Neville shares the story of how he got a divorce so he could marry his second wife in the lecture *Brazen Impudence* on September 27, 1968 he said, "When I decided to marry the lady who now bears my name I applied this principle. At the time I was terribly involved. I had married at the age of eighteen and became a father at nineteen. We separated that year, but I never sought a divorce; therefore, my separation was not legal in the state of New York. Sixteen years later, when I fell in love and wanted to marry my present wife, I decided to sleep as though we were married. While sleeping, physically in my hotel room, I slept imaginatively in an apartment, she in one bed and I in the other. My dancing partner did not want me to marry, so she told my wife that I would be seeking a divorce and to make herself scarce - which she did, taking up residence in another state. But I persisted! Night after night I slept in the assumption that I was happily married to the girl I love. Within a week I received a call requesting me to be in court the next Tuesday morning at 10:00 A.M.. Giving me no reason why I should be there, I dismissed the request, thinking it was a hoax played on me by a friend.

So the next Tuesday morning at 9:30 A.M. I was unshaved and only casually dressed, when the phone rang and a lady said: "It would be to your advantage, as a public figure, to be in court this morning, as your wife is on trial." What a shock! I quickly thanked the lady, caught a taxi, and arrived just as court began. My wife had been caught lifting a few items from a store in New York City, which she had not paid for. Asking to speak on her behalf I said: "She is my wife and the mother of my son. Although we have been separated for sixteen years, as far as I know she has never done this before and I do not think she will ever do it again. We have a marvelous son. Please do nothing to her to reflect in any way upon our son, who lives with me. If I may say something, she is eight years my senior and may be passing through a certain emotional state which prompted her to do what she did. If you must sentence her, then please suspend it."

The judge then said to me, "In all of my years on the bench I have never heard an appeal like this. Your wife tells me you want a divorce, and here you could have tangible evidence for it, yet you plead for her release." He then sentenced her for six months and suspended the sentence. My wife waited for me at the back of the room and said:"Neville, that was a decent thing to do. Give me the subpoena and I will sign it." We took a taxi together and I did that which was not legal: I served my own subpoena and she signed it.

Now, who was the cause of her misfortune? She lived in another state, but came to New York City to do an act for which she was to be caught and tried. So I say: every being in the world will serve your purpose, so in the end you will say: "Father forgive them, for they know not what they do." They will move under compulsion to do your will, just as my wife did. I tell this story only to illustrate a principle. You do not need to ask anyone to aid you in the answer to a prayer, for the simple reason that God is omnipotent and omniscient. He is in you as your own wonderful I Amness. Everyone on the outside is your servant, your slave, ready and able to do your will.

All you need do is know what you want. Construct a scene which would imply the fulfillment of your desire. Enter the scene and remain there. If your imaginal counselor (your feeling of fulfillment) agrees with that which is used to illustrate your fulfilled desire, your fantasy will become a fact. If it does not, start all over again by creating a new scene and enter it. It costs you nothing to imagine consciously! In my own case the scene was a bedroom of an apartment, with my wife in one bed and I in the other, denoting that I was no longer living in a hotel alone. I fell asleep in that state, and within one week I had the necessary papers to start action on a divorce. This is what the Bible teaches. It is my text book. 'Whatever you desire, believe you have already received it and you will!'"

Neville told a story of needing money and having loving mental conversations with Victor. He received the money without asking for it. On April 26, 1971 in the lecture *Control Your Inner Conversations* he said, "I tell you from my own experience, before the Promise was realized in me, seemingly I had this conversation with my brother.

Formerly I would argue mentally,—we were five thousand miles apart,—and I needed money at that time; and when I found myself arguing with him, I broke it—tore that entire record up. And whether he sent me a nickel or not, I loved him and praised him and thanked him, and went about my business, not knowing where the next was coming from, for I had spent a fortune by taking off one solid year and living at the same level that I had lived in previous years, and spent money like water. Then came that moment I needed money. And inwardly I carried on a conversation with him, and I thought that's a stupid thing to do; so I broke that record, and then I carried on the most glorious conversation with him, like two lovers, because I do love him and he loves me, And. I changed that "old man" into the "new man," by changing my conversation with him. Do you know, in no time flat—unasked, a very large wonderful check came to me? And no request; I didn't appeal at all.

I was "taking it out" on the one I loved because I myself had spent the money like a drunken sailor. And then here, inwardly, I am arguing with my brother; and when I broke it and actually carried on the most loving conversation with him—all about the family life and all these marvelous things, suddenly out of the nowhere came a very large, wonderful check. And I didn't appeal for it, So I am telling you from experience, I know it works this way."

Joseph Neville Goddard (5/19/1924 - 3/1/1986) was Neville's son with his first wife Mary. In world war two he was a marine on Guadalcanal. In the lecture *Conception* on March 11, 1968 Neville said, "Do you know you can put yourself into any state? My son actually put himself into the state of war by reading a book about Guadalcanal and falling in love with the pictures of the natives there! He certainly didn't enjoy his experiences while there, but he asked for it. You see: nothing happens by accident."

In 1943 after Neville got out of the Army he and his wife looked for a new apartment. On June 6, 1969 in the lecture *A Parabolic Revelation* he said, "Back in 1943 when I came out of the army I was looking for an apartment. My wife and I had determined how much we were going to pay for it, but when we found the apartment the rent was more than we had planned to pay. Realizing this, my wife said: "Well, that's not demonstrating this principle, is it?" I said nothing. I simply paid the months of September and October, but when I went to pay the November rent the manager said: "I have an apology to make to you. An authority of the city came in and looked over my books. He discovered that the apartment you have was formerly rented for less." Then he quoted the new rent figure to me, which was to the dollar the amount I had originally chosen to pay. It took me three months of being faithful to what I had imagined I was paying, even though during that time I was paying more. But, since the reduced rent was retroactive to the day I moved in, I got it all back at the beginning of the third month.

I committed myself in my imagination, to what I was going to pay. I went looking, and because I was going to pay more - in his eyes - he gave me all kinds of concessions he would not have done had I paid him what the former tenant did. First of all he allowed us to pick out the wallpaper, the colors and rooms we wanted painted. He even built a bookshelf for me which covered an entire wall, for all my books. He did everything I wanted; but if I had gone in there and gotten the rent for the amount I said I would pay, he would not have built the bookcase for me, given me the wallpaper, or painted the entire apartment to my specifications. Only then was the rent reduced to the amount I had imagined it to be, and we remained there almost fourteen years.

I tell you: imagination will not fail you if you are faithful. What could I say when I was confronted with the negation of my assumption? Nothing. I simply would not give up, and when the time was right my assumption became a fact. I urge you to set your goal high. Assume the feeling it has been reached and sleep in that feeling. Persist and I promise you that not one thing in this world can rob you of that which you have assumed."

In the lecture *The Duality Of Man* which occurred a little after October 20, 1964 because Neville said "like Mr. Hoover who just departed this world" in this lecture. That is the date that President Hoover died. Neville shares the story of getting his two brothers Victor and Lawrence tickets to see the opera Aida.

Neville said, "About eight years ago I was in New York for a month and two of my brothers, Victor and Lawrence, came up and spent two weeks with me in New York City, they checked into the same hotel. They wanted to see everything they could within two weeks and I bought them fourteen shows and sometimes they went even to an afternoon show. They wanted to see everything in the crowded two weeks. But the one thing my brother Lawrence wanted to see was the new presentation of Aida.

Well the papers said it was sold out from the very moment that it was stated a new presentation, same music naturally, the same score, but new scenery, something new about it. And this captured the imagination of all opera lovers as they all wanted to see Aida. The one thing he wanted to see was Aida but the papers had huge big ads, not one seat is available. Come down and buy a seat for the other shows and this was the old opera house around 40th Street and Broadway. It ran from Broadway to 7th, the old Metropolitan.

So, this morning we set out. I said, 'Now, It doesn't really matter.' I said, 'Let us go. We have to go down and have lunch anyway. We will go and just see.' We got there and huge big signs on the outside, no seats for Aida available and they were plastered all over the Metropolitan. I went in and there were three lines leading towards the three windows selling tickets for the entire season and there was no seats for Aida. I got into the first line. It was a very long line, then I saw the third line from me moving more rapidly than the first and the second so I moved over to that line.

Then they all moved rapidly forward as we got to the window and seemingly no hope of getting tickets, but before I left my hotel room I simply assumed that I had the tickets for my two brothers. I didn't want to go, they wanted to see it so I assumed that I gave them the tickets. I got into this line and it moved rapidly towards the window. As we got there, to the window, a tall blonde man, he was about, oh he must have been about six, I'm 5'11", he must have been about 6'4".

He stretched his hand up over my head and diverted the ticket seller as he asked the question, while one in front of me is buying, it's not for Aida for that's completely sold out, he is buying two other seats for some other opera. Then he departed after he diverted the man's attention and this man pushed on some bills under the window and then as the teller looked at the money; and this man is at the door now, the tall, tall blonde fellow. And he gave this man the ticket and then suddenly he said, 'well he only gave me three dollars. He should have given me' and he mentioned the money he should have given me.

At that he was bewildered. The teller was bewildered. I turned around and I screamed at that tall blonde, I said, 'Sir'. I screamed so loudly he couldn't stop but be attentive. He turned around. I said, 'Come back here, you're wanted.' He came back like a little child being led by the nose. He came back and he said, 'What's wrong?' And the man said, 'This is all that he gave me, two one dollar bills.' He said, 'Oh no he didn't, he gave you two tens.' and I said, 'No you didn't, I was standing right here. I saw what you did. You gave him two one dollar bills, that's all that you gave him.'

The man was flabbergasted. He was so completely dumbfounded he didn't know what to do. I said, 'I am standing here, I saw exactly what was done.' Then he opened up his purse and here was a stack of ones and he had a twenty dollar bill and two tens. He said to the man, 'When will you discover your mistake that I gave you two tens?' And the man said to him, 'At the end of the season.' And with that it was closed and the man then took out the money and paid for the ticket and took back his two ones.

Then I said to him, 'I want two seats for Aida tonight and I want them in the horseshoe circle. I want them center.' He said. 'Yes Sir.' and he took from what is called the VIP, they always keep a few out, though the house is sold out they always keep a few seats for those who are coming called very important people. Well, I am certainly not a very important person, but I saved him from the loss of twenty dollars and he quickly took the two seats out and said to me, 'Twenty dollars.' I gave him twenty dollars, went back and gave the two seats to my brothers.

Now, a state called a thief. These two men have chosen to be thieves in their world. They're con men, it's perfectly all right. God made everything for its purpose."

Neville talked about his health in the lecture *Imagination Fulfills Itself* on October 26, 1968 he said, "Now, I want to show you what I mean when I say you can be exactly what you want to be. Let me begin by telling you that for the last couple of months I have felt like the devil, yet I knew I was responsible for the hell I found myself in. The doctor gave me every possible test, and when I saw him yesterday he told me I was a dilemma.

Do you know what a dilemma is? It's an argument presenting two or more alternatives equally conclusive against an opponent. In other words, if you start on the assumption that whatever you choose your conclusion will be wrong, you have a dilemma. You can use anything as a dilemma. That's me. My blood indicated one thing in a certain test and the opposite in another. The tests only confirmed what I already knew: that the cause of my discomfort lay in the depth of my soul and not in any secondary cause - such as a thyroid, heart, liver, kidney, or anything outside of myself.

I am wearing a body, but it is not me. I put myself into this body, which limits me. I am its operant power. It cannot be causeful, as it only reflects what I am entertaining in my imagination. I must not justify it, condemn, or excuse myself in any way. Knowing I did not feel well, I changed my feeling, and when the tests (which I had taken to please the one I love) came back, I learned I was a dilemma."

On November 21, 1969 in the lecture *Enter The Dream* Neville said, "I was late getting here tonight. A friend came for lunch yesterday who, knowing the friend who brings me here every week, said: "Isn't he unreliable?" and I immediately answered, "No! Never." She didn't want to hear that and is a very intense lady who knows how to reach him. Today for the first time my friend called to say he couldn't make it. An intense imaginal act produced what the lady wanted to hear, but she will never get the satisfaction of hearing me say he was ever late or did not come.

There are people in this world whose surface veneer appears to be altogether wonderful, but below that surface there is an intensity and they do not know that they are only hurting themselves. She can't touch me, although undoubtedly she has tried; but if she did it would boomerang in a way she would not know. I love her dearly, but she is intense and also of the same school that if you are not of a certain physical background you are not 'in.'"

Neville talked about his dentist in the lecture *Secret Of Imagination* on June 21, 1971 he said, "In this audience tonight – and he may not even remember when he did it – is my dentist. I went to him in great need of a lot of work, but I have had dentistry all over this country and in London and Barbados, but it all was horrible. I was always on the move. I was with the theater. Getting in town for a week, what could they do when I needed such work? They patched me up. So, I met him. He gave me a complete job because I was here – living here then.

When one day a tooth gave way, which was an anchor tooth, he said to me quite innocently, whether he remembers it or not, "When I saw your mouth and did this, I said to myself, 'This tooth will last thirteen years.'

It was thirteen years. Had he only said 25, but he didn't think I would live that long! So, thirteen years – out came that anchor tooth, and therefore a complete restructure of my entire mouth. He set it in motion. Whether he remembers or not, he said, "This is going to last thirteen years." He didn't tell me; he didn't have to tell me. That was his imaginal act. I was only the victim of his creative power.

Now, I am telling you: Don't take anything lightly. You are creating morning, noon and night. Your imaginal acts are God's acts, because your imagination is God! And there is no other God…

But if I long after someone at that very moment the act was committed. I state it boldly. I state it boldly, as my dentist stated it boldly. It was committed. So, I went blindly on enjoying everything that he did. It was perfect. And suddenly comes a little bleeding thing, which no one could stop. Out comes the tooth. He set it in motion the day he said to himself – not to me: "It will last thirteen years." I checked it; it was thirteen years."

Famous People

Marian Anderson (2/27/1897 - 4/8/1993) was an African-American singer who in 1939 was denied to sing for an integrated audience at Constitution Hall in Washington D.C. by the Daughters of the American Revolution. On April 9, 1939 Easter Sunday, with the aid of Eleanor Roosevelt, she performed at the Lincoln Memorial for an integrated audience of 75,000 and a radio audience in the millions. In the lecture *Awake O Sleeper* on July 25, 1968 Neville said, "Here, Marian Anderson was denied the right to sing in the famous hall in Washington. She was not a member, and she was denied the right. She did not oppose it. She didn't fight it. These are her words. She said, "They had a right. These are the Daughters of the American Revolution. That was their right. They are all members of that club. They are proud of it. Why shouldn't they be proud of it? I simply would like to have sung in that hall. So, what did I do? I didn't fight it. I didn't argue it. I didn't tell the press. I made no issue. I simply in my imagination sang in that hall. I stood on that stage and sang to a full house –an appreciative house. They loved all that I did, and I was invited to sing in that hall."

Now you will say, "Well, Mrs. Roosevelt heard about it, and she then took issue with those who were the members, saying, "After all, this is tax-exempt property, and all of this is something that is on the backs of the taxpayer, and I feel that we should occasionally open the doors to some great artist." She might have given them any argument, and she was then the First Lady of the land. You will say,"Now that's why they invited Marion Anderson."

I say, "It was not." Mrs. Roosevelt had to act as she acted because Marion Anderson acted first, and if one could only see what she did –not what Mrs. Roosevelt did; she was only the means to the end. The cause of the entire thing was one who did not argue, who did not protest, who did nothing; who, in her own heart, simply imagined that she had done it. And if you do it this way, you don't have to fight in this world. You don't have to argue with anyone in this world. Just do it."

Robert Millikan (3/22/1868 - 12/19/1953) was an American experimental physicist and in 1923 he won the Nobel Prize for Physics. On April 26, 1971 in the lecture *Control Your Inner Conversations* Neville said, "Do what Robert Millikan did when he was a poor boy, and had nothing but a brilliant mind; a great, great understanding of literature; but he had no money, and he was tired of his poverty. And knowing how the mind works, he constructed a sentence that if true would imply he was no longer poor. And his sentence is a beautiful sentence; "I have,"—not "am going to have"—"I have a lavish, steady, dependable income, consistent with integrity and mutual benefit."

That was the great Robert Millikan, who was the head of Cal-Tech, who gave us his discovery of cosmic rays, who when he died could leave a fortune behind to these charities. I know that the YMCA was one of them; they got a fortune from him. He already settled on his sons and made them financially independent, but he had enough left over to give to his favorite charities, and lived a full, wonderful, marvelous life, where everyone who met him benefited by the actual meeting with that great man. And he started off from "scratch," using this simple technique - using the simple technique—using the gift of God that He gave to every person in this world: Mind and Speech."

Neville talked about an article that came out in 1957 about the three Kennedy's. In the lecture *The Source* on October 14, 1968 he said, "In the September 7, 1957 issue of the Saturday Evening Post, Harold H. Martin wrote an article entitled, "The Amazing Kennedys." In it he said: "Kennedy admirers look forward confidently to the day that they will see Jack in the White House, Bobby in the Cabinet as Attorney General, and Teddy as a senator from Massachusetts."

Here is a family who dared to break one of the most frightful barriers which ever existed in our country concerning the White House - to be a Catholic! My friend David always used the word, "WASP," (meaning White Anglo-Saxon Protestant), claiming that if you were not a WASP you could not seek the highest office in our land. Well, Kennedy was white, Anglo-Saxon, and Catholic. His entire family were ardent Catholics, yet they broke that barrier. Why? Because imagining creates reality.

Back in 1957, the imaginal acts of Kennedy admirers were printed for all to see. They did not say that Bobby would have a cabinet post, but specified what post! Or that Teddy would be a senator, but from which state he would represent - and it all came to pass. If it did not last, that is not the point; it came to pass! And because of the assassinations, their imaginal acts will remain indelibly impressed upon the history of our country. Lincoln, as well as those who are not important as presidents, live longer in the minds of men when they are assassinated. So here we find that ardent admirers, determining what they admired, persisted, and it came to pass. Why? Because the whole thing is within!...

Try to become as fervent of something for yourself as the Kennedy admirers were for him. Become as intense for self or a friend as they were for the family. Nothing was more impossible in our political setup than to be a Catholic and still aspire to the White House; but they did it and he got it and you can, too."

On July 25, 1968 in the lecture *Awake O Sleeper* Neville said, "No one wanted the White House more than Johnson, but he had to take a second place, but he got the White House, and not by election the first time. He went down to that convention convinced that he was going to get it, and then Kennedy got it. Kennedy lasted three years, and made his exit at the hand of the assassin, and then he stepped right into the breach within a matter of hours --well, minutes, really. Then he got the election on his own the second time. But no one wanted it more than he did."

Robert Kennedy was shot around midnight of June 5, 1968 and died the next day. In the lecture *There Is No Fiction* on June 7, 1968 Neville said, "You cannot feed the mind violence and not expect violence in the world. Although the networks will deny this, a friend at NBC-TV studio told me that when it was official that Kennedy was dead, he received an order from New York that for the next four days no violent films were to be shown. He said pandemonium took place in the studio, as they went through their files trying to find enough non-violent film to cover four days! Lucky for them, most of the time will be taken up with the giant coverage of the funeral in New York City.

One gentleman recently interviewed on television said that Senator Kennedy was always talking about being assassinated. That when the shots rang out, he instantly knew that Kennedy was dead. You cannot entertain thoughts of being assassinated without experiencing them. Who knows who, unseen by mortal eyes, was treading in the winepress, influencing that young boy's mind!...

Hearing of the success of another and feeling their joy builds a structure which will project itself on the screen of space. Calling the projection reality, one may think it was created from the outside. But what happened had to happen as it did, for there are no accidents. Last night Kennedy could have used other exits but he had to use the one he did, for there is a time for every imaginal act to project itself, just as there is a time to be born and a time to die, a time to laugh and a time to cry...

Think you are a martyr, and you are. And you will continue to be one until you change your thinking. The Kennedy's, believing they are martyrs, will have these blows repeated over and over again until they awaken from within. I don't care how good your life seems to be at the moment, it is a dream from which you must - and will - awaken."

On July 15, 1968 in the lecture *Who Am I?* Neville said, "My dear, I wouldn't say the boys suffered. The family left behind grieves, yes. We do not ever recognize our own hearts. No one knows the thought of a man, but the spirit of man who dwells in him. Likewise, no man knows the thoughts of God, but the Spirit of God who dwells in Him. Who knows what thought those boys entertained? The three of them were killed violently, and so was a sister. Joseph was killed in the war. His sister was killed, her husband was killed, and these two boys were assassinated. Who knows what thoughts they entertained? To be dramatic, I do not know. In other words, everything was done when the first was assassinated to identify his name with Lincoln – the same feeling – not McKinley, but he was assassinated too. But they tried to make it a Lincoln fiction, to set it for the future, and they've done it. So, if you want glory on earth, they certainly have it. They have it if you want it on earth; but all the things of earth will vanish, and leave not a trace behind them. Everything here is going to pass away as though it never were; and all will awaken."

Martin Luther King Jr. (1/15/1929 - 4/4/1968) was a Baptist minister and prominent civil rights leader who was assassinated on April 4, 1968. Neville shares an interview he read with Mrs. King in the lecture *The Identical Harvest* on July 13, 1970 he says, "Recently I read an interview with Mrs. Martin Luther King, the widow of the great evangelist, and she said the day that the late President Kennedy was assassinated, "My husband turned to me and said, "That is the way I am going to die. I, too, will be assassinated." He was a powerfully emotional being; he identified himself with that martyrdom. Whether he wanted to be a martyr for his own cause or not, I do not know. But her own words, "My husband said to me when he heard of the story of the assassination of Kennedy, 'That's the way I am going to be killed. I am going out just like that.'"

Now, you tell that man that he did it, and the one who now serves 99 years was only the means by which his will was externalized, he would not believe it. There's always somebody ready, waiting to aid the externalization of my will, and my will is a simple imaginal act – that's all; and, then, you, if you can be used; if you are not in that state that you can be used, you will not be used against your will. But there are those who are falling into all kinds of states in this world. There are those who feel at home being a thief. Well, if I feel that I have lost something, the states occupied by men who believe themselves to be thieves, they will fulfill my will for me. If I feel that I am secure, there are those in the world who will play their part and aid the birth of my feeling that I am secure. It's entirely up to us. What are we doing?"

Clifton Webb (11/19/1889 - 10/13/1966) was an actor, singer, and dancer from 1913 - 1962. Neville mentions him in the lecture *Awake O Sleeper* on July 25, 1968 he said, "I read here, oh, maybe eight or ten years ago the famous men in the theatrical world whose mothers always looked upon them as most important. Clifton Webb was one whose mother, from the time he was a little baby, treated him as most important, and they mentioned about eight or ten or twelve of them. Each rose to stardom in the theatrical world, because they had mothers who treated them in a different manner. And, so, the story came out in the magazine I read. I know it's only based upon a single law, if the mothers knew it. Well, whether they knew it or not, that's how they acted, and it's simply putting into effect God's Law."

William Butler Yeats (6/13/1865 - 1/28/1939) was an Irish writer and poet. He received a Nobel Prize for Literature in 1923. On May 31, 1971 in the lecture *God Given Talent* Neville said, "Now, let me share with you a few stories. These stories by William Butler Yeats – you can find them in his volume called "Good and Evil." They first came out at the turn of the Century. It is part of his collective works, but this individual volume has been reprinted, I think, three or four times, and this is the chapter which he named "Magic." He said: 'I was spending a vacation in Paris, and I got up early. I thought I would go out and get the morning paper before my host rose, and then I came through, and

I saw the little maid laying the table for breakfast, and I told myself one of those long, stupid stories that one tells only to oneself.

If something could happen which had not happened, I would have hurt my arm, and so I imagined myself with my arm in a sling. As I passed by, I had so completely imagined myself with my arm in a sling that I cast my imaginal act upon that sensitive child – the little girl who was simply preparing the breakfast table. When I returned with my paper, my hostess met me at the door, and she was all in a dither, inquiring about my arm, for she said that the little girl, the maid, had told her that Mr. Yeats came down with his arm in a sling. Then I remembered what I had done. I simply imagined that had I done what I had not done, I would have hurt my arm, and my arm would now be in a sling, so I cast my imaginal act so intensely upon that maid that she saw it as an actual fact."

"Now," he said, "just about the same time I thought intensely of a fellow student and a message I wanted to give him, but I did not wish it committed to paper. I wanted to tell it to him, but he was not present. Two days later I got a letter from this fellow student who was several hundred miles away, and just about the time that I had intensely thought of him and the message, I appeared, seemingly, in bodily form, as though in the flesh, in a large hotel where he was amidst a large crowd of people and he told me that he would like me to return after the crowd was gone, and then I vanished and returned that night at midnight and told him the message, which he told me in his letter."

"Now," he said, "I have no conscious knowledge of the projection. I only know that I intensely thought of my fellow student and the message I wanted to convey, and there I appeared in the midst of a huge crowd in a hotel several hundred miles away, and he was telling me to return later after the crowd dispersed, which I did at midnight, and told him the message. "Now," he said, "I could tell you unnumbered stories of the power of imagination."

Then he tells the one of Joseph Blanco, which is a popular story and supposedly very, very true, of this student at Oxford University finding himself – well, without funds, so he could not continue his studies, so the day that he left college because he could not afford to continue he found no job, and he joined himself to a bunch of gypsies – traveling gypsies. And one day two students who knew him at college came upon him among the gypsies, and he made a sign not to be identified, and then came up afterwards, and he told them, "I'll meet you at the inn, and then I will explain to you why you find me among this crowd."

Well, they were curious and went to the inn, and when he came into the inn, he told them that they are not quite the vagabonds that people think they are. They have a secret that is not known at Oxford, "none of our professors know it. I know I never heard about it," said he, "so no one knows it, but I will tell you what they have taught me. I have learned all that they have taught me so far, and I have improved upon it. Now to show you what I mean by it, I will leave you two fellows alone, and when I return I will tell you what you have discussed in my absence."

So, when he came back, he told them in detail what they had discussed, everything they had discussed, and they were curious, and wondered why. He said, 'You had no choice in the matter. I determined what you would discuss. My imagination led yours. Their story is all about imagination, and they, by the complete control of their own imagination, influence your behavior. That's what I learned from them.'"

David Moses is an actor who got his big break in 1969 and as of 2022 is still working. In 2022 he is Marty on *Bosch: Legacy* and has many movie and tv roles in his long career. In the lecture *The Rock* on February 19, 1969 Neville talked about David. The pilot that is mentioned was for the tv show *The New People* in the role of Gene Washington. Neville said, "A friend recently shared this experience with me. A few years ago his friend was about to give up the theater, believing it was too difficult for him - a black man - to succeed. My friend loaned him my book, Out Of This World, in which I stated that an assumption, though false, if persisted in, would harden into fact. His friend read the book but could not believe this statement.

Then one day I autographed a book for this gentleman with these words of Blake: "If the fool will persist in his folly he will become wise." This gentleman's name is David Moses. When he received that book it did something to him, for he began to persist in the folly of claiming success even though the evidence of his senses denied it.

Within a matter of weeks he received an offer for the Greyhound commercial. From that he received movie and TV contracts. He is scheduled to be on the Dianne Carroll show and has just completed a pilot for Danny Thomas, who told him that the show, when accepted by the network, would start this coming September with either twenty-six or thirty-nine segments. Here is one who dared to persist in his dream...

In the case of the gentleman I told you about, he is now a success and may perhaps forget how his success came to be. Quite often when people reach their goal they turn their back on the ladder by which they did ascend and forget the God who gave it birth! I hope this gentleman remembers, because no one gets off the wheel of recurrence until he is judged perfect by the one who began the good work in him. Only then will the individual become superimposed upon the Son of God to form the one God and Father of all."

That which I have done, I have done! Do nothing!

This chapter is about how Neville was drafted and got out of the Army. He talked about Colonel Theodore Bilbo, Jr. (6/22/1910 - 8/30/1979) who was the Battalion Commander of the 490th Armored Field Artillery of the 11th Armored Division Artillery. In the middle of October 1944 they landed in England and Colonel Bilbo was then assigned as Executive Officer of Combat Command A (CCA), under Brig Gen. Willard A. Holbrook, Jr. He served in the Army for 30 years. His father was Theodore Gilmore Bilbo (10/13/1877 – 8/21/1947) who was a Democrat that served as a two time Governor (1916-20, 1928-32) and a US Senator (1935 - 1947) representing Mississippi.

In the lecture *The Perfect Law Of Liberty* on April 2, 1971 Neville said, "Well, I was drafted into the Army, seventeen millions of us. Well, I didn't ask the permission of any one, I only consulted myself. I looked around, and I knew what the world knows: it was something that had to be done. But I must be honest with myself. I didn't want any part of it, but no part of it! Others would tell me, "Is that the act of a coward?" I didn't care what they said – "Is that being a good citizen?" I didn't care what they said. As I just said earlier, what we now know, which is called Reason – it's a reasonable thing to do; we are at war, and we are all Americans. We should be going there because our country has declared war – go in there and fight. And so, Reason tells us that should be done.

When I was drafted, I did not oppose it. They drafted me. They took me down to Camp Polk, Louisiana, for my basic training, and while I was there, I didn't want any part of it, and I dared to assume that I'm out of it. I made my normal, natural application, as you have to do in the world of Caesar. Within 24 hours it came back, and it was simply rejected. It was signed, "Disapproved," and signed by my Colonel, a very nice gentleman. His name was Colonel Theodore Bilbo, Jr. His father was Senator from Mississippi. I said nothing.

My Captain said, "For your sake, Goddard, I am very, very sorry. I know exactly how you feel. You want to be with your wife and little girl. Your son is in Guadalcanal with the Marines, and you are now almost 38, and so I know, but I would like to go through this war with a man just like you at my side. So, I can't say that I am sorry for myself; I am sorry only for you."

I didn't say one word to him, or to the Colonel; I didn't oppose it. That was the decision of Caesar. Now I looked into the perfect law, the Law of Liberty, and I persevered in that law; and I slept that night as though I slept in my own home in New York City on Washington Square, where I lived on the 7th floor. I lived on that floor; it was a very large apartment – two bedrooms, a lovely big living room, a dining room, a huge kitchen, and the foyer; and I slept in that place just as though I were there and not in the Army. I fell asleep in that state, having done all the normal things that would make me feel this arrangement is perfect. I rearranged the structure of my mind. Instead of seeing 25 men around me sleeping upstairs and knowing that there were 25 down below in the next area, I slept in my own bed with my wife in her bed and my little girl in her crib in the corner. I felt everything in that place just as though it's taking place, and I rearranged the structure of my mind, and fell sound asleep in that state.

At 4:00 o'clock in the morning, here comes a sheet of paper before my eyes and a hand from here down [indicating], with a pen in its hand; and the pen scratched out the word "disapproved," and it wrote in, in a bold script, "Approved." And then I heard the words: "That which I have done, I have done. Do nothing!" And then I awoke. It was too early to disturb the 25 other fellows sleeping there, and I waited until the very first moment that I could leave that room, and went down to the latrine and shaved and bathed early, and came up filled with a glow that the whole thing was done. I walked in that assumption for the next nine days.

Nine days later, the same Colonel that disapproved my request called me in. He said, "Close the door, Goddard." So, I closed the door. He said, "Take a seat." He never asked me to take a seat in his presence before. I was a Private. You always stood in his presence, and never took a seat. Then he gave me all the reasons in the world why I should still be in the Army. He said, "Do you still want to get out?"

I said, "Yes, Sir."

He gave me another reason. "Do you still want to get out?"

I said, "Yes, Sir."

Another one; and when he exhausted all the reasons why I should be in the Army, I was still saying, "Yes, Sir."

He said, "All right, bring me another application and have your Captain sign it," which I did. And that day I was honorably discharged and out of the Army. I didn't run away; I was honorably discharged.

"When vision breaks forth into speech, the presence of Deity is assured," and who can oppose God? He said, "That which I have done, I have done. Do nothing!"

So, he thought he initiated the urge to let me go free. I looked into the perfect law, the Law of Liberty, and I persevered in that law; and he played his part, for I rearranged the structure of my mind.

I was convinced I wanted out, and I didn't ask anyone's permission. I did not discuss it with anyone as to why I should want out when seventeen million are being drafted, plus numberless girls to make a tremendous effort against this monstrous thing that was going on in Europe. I still wanted out. I did not take anyone into my confidence as to why I wanted out. I had my 13 weeks basic training, and then when I came out, they gave me my citizenship papers. Back in 1922 I could have been an American, but I just didn't have the time or the urge to get around to become a citizen; so I drifted on and drifted on and drifted on until after this little episode. That's why I went into the Army, or I would still be drifting through, being a citizen of Britain. But now I'm an American by adoption. And they gave it to me because I did fulfill a 13-week training course in the American Army.

So, I tell you, I know from experience how true this statement in James is. Read it carefully. "Be doers of the word, and not hearers only, deceiving yourself. For he who is a hearer of the word, and not a doer, he is like one who looks into the mirror and sees his natural face; and then he goes away and at once forgets what he looks like. But he who is a doer, he looks into the perfect law, the Law of Liberty, and perseveres. And when he does that, he is blessed in his doing."

That is, acting – making the thing become alive within you. Now, he tells us in the same chapter? "Faith without works is dead, as the body, apart from the spirit, is dead, so faith without works is dead."

He is not proposing that I substitute works for faith. Works are the evidence whether the faith I profess is alive or dead. I say I believe the story of Scripture. Well then, if I believe it, then do it!

He said, "Whatever you desire, believe you have received, and you shall."

If I really believe that – I can't say I believe by quoting the Apostle's Creed. That's not belief. Going to church and genuflecting before some man-made little cross – that's not Scripture. Do you really believe the doctrines, the teachings, of Scripture? Not the traditions of men, not the rituals, not the outer ceremonies; but the teachings of Scripture – "When you pray, believe that you have received, and you will." And, "All things are possible to him who believes." Well, do I believe that? Well then, believe it!

If I really believe that I am out of the Army, what and where would I be? Well, I would be at home, in my place a thousand miles away, on Washington Square. If I looked through the window, I would see the Holly Apartments, if I looked to the left, I would see Washington Square, if I looked to the right, I would see Sixth Avenue – it's now called "the Avenue of the Americas"; but then– and still is to me, raised as I was there, – it's still Sixth Avenue to me. And there I would look at Sixth Avenue. Well, I did that, that night. I saw Sixth Avenue, I saw Washington Square, and then I went through the entire apartment and touched objects with my imaginary hands.

Now, was that rational? The world would say that was the most irrational thing that one can do. Now, what is reason? The office of reason is simply to extract conclusions from premises.

Must my premises always be based upon the evidence of my senses? Must they always dictate what is rational to me? Well, having done this, and proved it to be a fact, reason doesn't mean to me what it means to the world. For, they would sleep in the Army; and I wrote a friend of mine who was a Freudian, and he practiced psychiatry in New York City. He was drafted – he was an Englishman, too, and he was drafted, and he was off in Florida – a man my age.

So, when I got out, knowing exactly what I did, I wrote him a detailed letter telling him what I did, and how to do it. No – he was a Freudian, and that was something that didn't make sense to him. To him, the whole thing was centered in sex, not in this use of the imagination. All right, he didn't answer my letter. I got out in 1943 in the spring, in the month of April – March or April of 1943. They drafted me November the 19th, 1942, and I got out in March 1943.

When the war was over and all the other fellows were being discharged, he was discharged, and he said to me afterwards, "You know, Neville, I love to come to your lectures and to hear you because it's interesting. It's fairy. You turn my daily bread into the substance of fairy, but while I listen to you, you know what I do? I put my feet right down into the carpet, and I hold onto the sides of the chair to keep my sense of the reality and the profundity of things."

Well, he kept on holding to his little cot in the Army for another three years because he couldn't let go and put himself where he wanted to be. So, I am telling you how it's done. I am telling you how it's done from my own experiences that my perceptions are not necessarily bounded by organs of perception. I perceive more than sense, no matter how acute they are, could discover. My senses couldn't discover what I am seeing. Only in my imagination could it be done. I'm seeing the Holly Apartments, I am seeing Sixth Avenue, I am seeing Washington Square, I am seeing the bed, my wife, my child. I hadn't seen them in three months, but they are all there. I didn't bring sex into it. No – I didn't go to bed with her. There she was – the girl I loved, she was in her own bed, and I in my own bed. We have twin beds. And my little girl was then just over a year – not quite a year. She was born in June of 1942; this was not yet June of 1943, so she was not yet a year old. Here is my sweet little child, Vicki, in her bed. And I walked through the entire thing and touched all the objects, and felt them so normal and so natural, and came back to my bed and slept in it.

If any one was sensitive in that room, they would have seen me sleeping there. I was so natural to myself, they would have seen me – actually seen me there.

And then the next day, he had a change of mind but he couldn't act upon it. He was resisting the change, but, "That which I have done, I have done. Do nothing!" So, he resisted it for nine days, and they called me in and told me to bring a new application, which I did. And that day I was out."

In the July 25, 1968 lecture *Awake O Sleeper* Neville mentioned the regulation that any man over 38 years old was eligible for a discharge from the Army. He said, "I went to the Colonel. I was 38 years old, and in the Army, and a regulation came down from Washington that any man over 38 was eligible. It didn't say he would get it, but he was eligible for discharge. That rested purely with his commanding officer. He could not appeal it to the divisional commander. It has to rest with the battalion commander.

Well, I went to my battalion commander. He allowed as much as: Yes, you are 38 years old, and therefore you can apply, so I applied. Four hours later it was sent back to my company commander – the captain, and the captain called me in and said, "I am sorry for your sake, Goddard, but the Colonel has disallowed it," and he showed it to me. So I saw the signature and saw the paper. I didn't protest for the simple reason, you couldn't. This is the Army, and you can't go beyond what they say is the regulation. So, the battalion commander had the final word. If he felt he needed me in the Army – why, I wouldn't know but he thought he did, and so he said, No. That night I simply slept in my imagination in New York City, almost two thousand miles away, for I was down in Camp Polk, Louisiana; and here I'm sleeping on Washington Square in New York City, and that night, in my imagination, as I told you earlier, this is what happened. I still did nothing. Nine days later he calls me in, and after he gives me a tongue lashing for wanting to get out, he said, "Do you still want to get out?" I said, "Yes, Sir." You can't just say Yes to the Colonel, so I "sirred" him to death –Yes, Sir. Yes, Sir. Yes, Sir. Yes, Sir. "You still want to get out?" "Yes, Sir." "Do you know the best dressed man in this country today is the man who wears the American uniform?" I said, "Yes, Sir." "You still want to get out?" I said "Yes,Sir." And I kept on "yessing" him to death, and then he got up and signed a piece of paper. He said, "Sign that other form," and then that evening I was honorably discharged, and he came out to me – a nice chap – a big, tall, strapping fellow, and put his hand forward and he said, "Goddard, I will meet you in New York City after we" – and the emphasis was on we – "have won this war." I said, "Yes, Sir." No regrets.

So I went off to my train and to New York City. He was doing his job. If I had to be in the Army, I would like to follow a man like that. He was a real leader – no question about it. I don't imagine that man would have asked me to do something that he himself would not willingly do. I don't believe he would. He was a real man – Colonel Theodore Bilbo, Jr."

Neville mentioned that his sense of touch was the strongest; in the lecture *The State Of Vision* on February 26, 1968 he said, "You can raise any sense - be it hearing, sight, sound, touch or smell - to the state of vision. I was drafted into the army during World War II, but I wanted no part of it. When my request for a discharge was disapproved, I did not get angry and try to go over the colonel's head. Instead, I lay down on my army cot, closed my eyes to the other fifty men in the room, and imagined I was two thousand miles away in my apartment above Washington Square in New York City. Placing myself on my bed, I saw my wife sleeping in hers. Then I rose, and looking out the window, I saw the Holly Apartments across the street and Washington Square down below. Turning, I walked into the living room, dining room, and the kitchen. I felt familiar objects and brought as many of my five senses alive in the drama as possible. At 4:00 o'clock in the morning I awoke hearing a voice say, "That which I have done, I have done. Do nothing." Who spoke those words? I did, but I heard them as coming from without.

Knowing what I had done and what I had said, I walked in faith for nine days, doing nothing on the outside. On the tenth day the colonel who had rejected my application called me into his office and gave me an honorable discharge.

I brought feeling up to the state of vision. By feeling the bed and the various objects in the apartment, I fell asleep feeling the joy of being there. The colonel thought he initiated the desire to discharge me, but he had no choice in the matter. I imagined, knowing the world was my imagination pushed out, and everyone in it had to do what they are doing to aid the birth of what I had done...

Start now to exercise your God-given talents of sight, sound, touch, taste, and smell - together, or individually. The sense of touch is the strongest in me. If someone expresses their desire to me in a letter, I touch the paper they wrote, believing they are telling me of their desire's fulfillment. I know only one out of ten ever respond after I have granted their request, but that is all right. Having felt their letter and seen its contents, I know I have impregnated myself with the good fortunes they are desiring, and in so doing, my own captivity is being lifted."

In the lecture *The Game Of Life* on March 7, 1969 he said, "In your desire to go anywhere you must first go there in your imagination, and even those who may deny your request will aid you when the time is right. I got out of the army that way. Knowing I wanted to be honorably discharged and in my apartment in New York City, I slept as though it had already happened and I was already there. Then my captain - who had previously disallowed my discharge - had a change of heart and aided in my release. Anyone can do it. This game is easy to play and can be lots of fun in the doing. Think of an object you would like to hold. Think of a place you would desire to be. Then find an object in that room and feel it until it takes on sensory vividness.

Don't make it a lamp, but that lamp; not a table, but that table. Sit in that chair until you feel the chair around you. View the room from that chair and you are there, for you are all imagination and must be wherever you are in your imagination. Now, cast your bread upon the water by feeling the relief of being there, and let your genie - who is your slave - build a bridge of incident over which you will cross to sit in that chair, hold that lamp, and touch that table"

Neville shared a story about sending his friend, who also was in the Army, a letter explaining how he got out. In the lecture *The Flood Is Still Upon Us* he said, "When in March of 1943, by using my Imagination to penetrate the fact I, too, was in "prison" in the Army, but I didn't want any part of it. So, I simply penetrated the fact and saw myself in New York City, in my own apartment with my family. And in nine days I was out, honorably discharged, in my apartment in New York City.

I wrote a friend of mine who was in the army. He was my age. He was a Freudian, – a professional psychoanalyst, but Freud was his background. That was his schooling. When I wrote him in detail exactly what I had done (I didn't mince matters; I told him exactly what I did): as I physically slept on my little bed in the barracks, I imagined I was simply elsewhere. The "elsewhere" was a definite spot in space: New York City, in my apartment. I told him what I did. I could "feel" the bed. I could "feel" the things in my house. I went about feeling all the familiar objects in my apartment, and I gave it all the tones of reality and all the sensory vividness to the best of my ability. I "touched" everything, and it felt real, and then I went back to sleep. Then I told exactly what happened to me that morning; and then nine days later, I was honorably discharged by the same man who had disallowed my application.

He didn't answer my letter. In New York City he used to come to my meetings as a friend because he was so convinced that the Freudian concept was true. He said: "I come to your meetings for this reason, Neville ..." (We knew each other well. He'd come home for dinner; I'd go to his place for dinner) ... but he said: "I come to your meetings because you turn my daily bread into the substance of fairy. I sort of like that," he said. "But when I listen to you I hold the chair and I put my feet right firmly on the ground to feel the reality and the profundity of things. You aren't going to take me away with you. You are going to leave me right here where things are solidly real, so I feel the place under my foot and I feel the things next to my hands. I hold on tightly while you weave your story concerning moving off in one's imagination." He would not penetrate the facts. So, when did he get out? When the other millions got out. So he remained with his facts for the next three years! I got out in March of 1943; he came home to New York City in 1946, demobilized as the other millions and millions of boys were. He could not let go [of] the facts. This is the flood – there is no other flood – this is the flood. We are "drowned" with facts, victimized by them...

Then the promise is made: "Wherever the sole of your foot shall stand, that I have given to you." (Deuteronomy 11:24) I am not going to make you a promise and not fulfill it; I'll give it to you if you can stand upon it. So, I actually "stood" upon my apartment; I actually stood upon that floor and I felt the bed. I felt everything and gave it reality. My friend wouldn't allow himself to sleep in one place and assume that he was sleeping elsewhere, because that is a divided state of mind. He didn't want to become a split personality. So, he wanted to be completely coordinated. Well, he was coordinated all right, for the next three years, all in one little spot in his barracks. And for three years he couldn't get out, because – first of all – he wouldn't try it, because I turned his "daily bread into the substance of fairy." So he did not answer my letter. I have reminded him a few times since: "Why didn't you answer the letter?"

"Well, first of all, it didn't make sense, and I don't believe," said he, "that really what you did was the sole cause of your discharge." He always questioned it. Then I'd repeat it another time and tell him again what happened this time. "Well, that would have happened anyway." Then you do it a third time and you do it a fourth time. Do you know: if you did it a thousand times he would still say: "Do it once more." It will always happen, as far as they are concerned. It just didn't happen because you did something; these things would have happened anyway. I asked: "Why do you analyze people then and let things happen?"

"We are not the creatures of circumstance," said a man who bears your name, for his first name is Israel; and Disraeli's name is simply "of Israel" – Benjamin Disraeli. He said: "Man is not the creature of circumstances; circumstances are the creatures of men." He knew how to create things all in his imagination.

So I said: "You bear the name of Israel, but you don't apply the story of Israel. If you'd only apply it ... why, these things are taught us in Scripture." Scripture is not secular history; this is contemporary. It didn't happen thousands of years ago. The Flood is on! This is the Flood. The whole vast world is inundated with "facts," like the prominent papers, the evening paper, "The Examiner," and they are proud of the fact that they only print "facts." They don't embellish it – no frills, only the facts."

In the lecture *Awake O Sleeper* on July 25, 1968 Neville added, "Another chap, when I got out of the Army by the application of this law, without hurting anyone – honorably discharged, I wrote a friend of mine who was in the Army. He's a Freudian, and he teaches it. Now he's in L.A. So I wrote him exactly what I did. I did not hurt anyone. I didn't go A.W.O.L. I was called in and honorably discharged by the very man who said to me, "No. I disapprove." My Colonel. The same one called me in and approved it, and I didn't raise a finger. I simply applied it –applied the law. So, I told him. He ignored me completely –wouldn't answer my letter.

So, he remained in for the duration, and he got out at the end as the other millions got out, but he used to come to my meetings in New York City, and one day he said to me, "You know, Neville, I love coming and listening to you. It interests me. But you know what I do? I stick my feet into the carpet, and I hold onto the sides of my chair to keep my sense of profundity and the reality of things. You turn my daily bread into the substance of theory. I'll have none of it." He wants to be right down here on earth. Well, he was there on earth for the entire duration. I told him what I did.

A simple, simple thing: I went to bed in the barracks, with all the other men around me, and I dared to assume that I was home in New York City, and that right before my eyes came that same sheet of paper –or similar –that my Colonel had sent back saying, "Disapproved." And it came down this way, and then a hand from here – I didn't see the face; I saw the hand, and the hand took a pen and scratched out the word "Disapproved" and boldly wrote in script, "Approved." And a voice said to me, "That which I have done, I have done. Do nothing." I awoke. I was wearing this watch that my wife gave me when I was drafted. It was 4:15. I did nothing. At the end of nine days the Colonel calls me in, and I was honorably discharged, and that same signature – his name was Bilbo, Colonel Theodore Bilbo, Jr. – his father was Senator from Mississippi. And that's my experience. So, with the experience, I am sharing it with a friend, but he wouldn't take it."

Friends

Freedom Barry (1921 - 2014) was given Neville's book *Your Faith Is Your Fortune* and read it. He wanted to find more books by Neville and was told that Neville had moved to Los Angeles; that he had lectures on Mondays and Thursdays at the Wilshire and he could find the books there. He went to the lectures to buy a book and then left without going in to see the lecture. He did that until after he bought and read all of Neville's books and then he went into the lectures to see Neville speak. He went to all the lectures in Los Angeles and gave Neville his own success stories using the Law. Neville was asked to do more lectures in San Francisco than he could do so he asked Freedom if he would take his San Francisco mailing list and do some lectures which started his own speaking career.

In the lecture *All Powerful Human Word* on June 5, 1970 Neville said, "Now we will start with a story that happened this past week. A very dear friend of mine that I persuaded to do this work in San Francisco – you know him, Freedom Barry. He now lives in Cambria. That is halfway between here and San Francisco. He has one consuming passion, and that's music. He graduated from the New England Conservatory of Music, but he felt that he was not equal to the concert field. It is highly competitive, and he really felt that he was not quite of that timber. He was born and raised in poverty – extreme poverty. He was an orphan when he was simply a little child – a little baby. Well, he came west and got a job, and when he came to my meetings, after about two years I met him. I rather liked him, and I asked him if he would like to do what I am doing, and he said, "Yes, I would, but I am not qualified."

I said, "You only answered correctly. If you felt you were qualified, you'd be no earthly good."

Today, I would say I am not qualified. If you asked me for my intellectual background, I couldn't qualify: ask me for any background,

I couldn't qualify. I once met Damrosch in New York City at the Bohemian Club. At the HarvardClub they met once a month. And when I was introduced to him by this most outgoing person, he asked me what was my background. Was it Germanic as far as my teaching? Was it Germanic, was it French, was it English? I said, No, it all came by revelation; and the old man turned his back on me as though he was talking to the scum of the earth!

Here was a social gathering. He judged you by your background, based upon whether you were trained in the Germanic school, the French school, the English school, and he named it. Well, I could not have answered in the affirmative that question; so he turned his back.

So, I said to Freedom, "You do not need any background. You trust me. I like you. I think you are honest, and you will not deceive anyone. You will go north and you will teach."

So he went north and he has been teaching successfully. He bought himself a home in Cambria, as I said, midway between here and San Francisco. It's a modest home, but at least it's his home. It's all clear. But there is one consuming passion that he has; it's music. He loves music, and he had this lovely grand piano, but something was needed. He had to have it, not repaired, but something must be done, and there was a moderate charge of $400 to do what he thought should be done, but they could only do it if he sent it back to the factory. It was sent to the factory.

They would not ship it back to him unless he first came down and tested it and tried it out. Everything ought to be just right as he thought it to be right. So he came down, played on it, and he accepted it. Then they gave him a date of delivery. So he waited at home, but there was no piano. The next day, no piano.

Then he called them, and they said, "Well, we were waiting for a full load; but now there is a full load, and so you will get your piano Wednesday" – of last week – not this week, Wednesday of last week. He waited in all day and there was no piano; so then when he called, they said strangely enough, "Our driver and the truck and its contents have disappeared and we cannot locate him. We cannot locate the truck or the contents."

The next day when he called, there was no trace of the driver. So, in desperation, he called me. He said, "You know, I teach this Law but Neville every penny that I have is really locked up in my piano. I have my home but I have no income at the moment and my one outgoing thing is simply to play. And it's only insured for $2,000, and I could not replace it for $4,000. But long before I could get the $2,000, if ever, here I am strapped; and I am calling you to help. You are the only one to whom I can turn."

I said, "Thank you for the confidence"; and then that was it.

Right after I hung up, I heard him play that piano. I could put my hands upon his shoulder, and I could feel Freedom. I could feel the piano, and I heard this lovely music. Then that night between 8:00 and 10:00 there is a lovely program that comes on KFAC, and it's usually piano music, but it is lovely music all through the day, 24 hours a day. So any time of the day I can turn that on, which is really turned on all day anyway. And I heard this glorious concerto, and I imagined Freedom was playing it, and I simply put my hands upon him and thanked him for the joy he gave me in the playing of this concerto, and I could feel the piano.

Yesterday morning at 11:00 o'clock he called. I was not available but my wife answered. He said, "I would have called you at 4:30 this morning when the piano was delivered, but I thought it unwise to disturb you at that hour in the morning, at 4:30; but now I am going to call you, because you must be up." He said, "I am going to give you all the details eventually, I can't do it now over the phone. It was a strange, strange thing."

He did say this much: the driver was arrested in San Luis Obispo. He refused to give anything concerning the whereabouts of the truck and its contents.

Only this past week I read in the paper that our banks lose from men who hold up the banks –oh, maybe seven or eight million dollars a week, but the embezzlement that goes on within the banks from trusted employees runs into tens of millions; and then this enormous hundreds of millions between our ports, airports and warehouses in lost cargo –all stolen. A man takes off, and everything disappears, the truck and its contents; and it runs into hundreds and hundreds of millions of dollars a year.

But I don't care what I read in the paper. I am remaining faithful to Principle. There is one infallible statement concerning the unforgivable sin. The unforgivable sin in the Bible is the sin against the Holy Spirit. Every sin in the world is forgiven but the sin against the Holy Spirit. What is that unforgivable sin? Doubt! He who created the universe and sustains it, and you doubt His power to do anything in this world? That is the one unforgivable sin.

Well, having reached the end of God's plan for all of us, I will not doubt. I did not ask Freedom anything beyond his request. He wanted his piano, and all that I did – I simply heard him play it. I put my hands – my mental hands, my imaginary hands–on his shoulder and thanked him for the joy I got from hearing him play it. And then when I turned on KFAC between 8:00 and 10:00 and heard this delightful piano concerto, I assumed it was Freedom playing it; and I so enjoyed the master who played it that I thanked him for the joy of having heard it, and then I dropped it.

Now I am waiting for the details, but I do not really concern myself with how it happened. In spite of the hundreds of millions of dollars that are lost every year and never recovered, that did not faze me for one moment. He had his piano back –that is all that mattered, and so I simply lost myself in that act, and that was it."

Neville adds a little more detail in the June 8, 1970 lecture *The Pattern Of Scripture Is Real* he said, "As I told you the story at the last lecture what I did with my friend Freedom, it was quite simple to me just to "hear" him play and to put my hands on his shoulders and to thank him for the joy he gave me in that wonderful piano concerto. I did it three times in the interval of one week, and then he called to tell me the piano came back. Here, the average person would not have given him one dollar for the return of that piano, for at the moment unnumbered things are stolen between the pick-up and the delivery. And the truck disappeared, the contents disappeared, the driver disappeared. I have not heard from Freedom since, to get the details; but he did say when he first called, they have found the driver in San Luis Obispo, but he refused to give them any news concerning the truck or its contents. So, they put him in jail, and had to keep him there for five days before they could bring action because that's the law, but they put him in jail for five days. Now, why he confessed where the truck was, I do not know, but nevertheless he confessed, and they finally got Freedom's piano. So he has it back.

I only know what I did. I do not know anything concerning the case, other than what I did after he called me. I merely assumed the feeling of the wish fulfilled; and to do it, in my mind's eye, I saw him sitting at the piano. I "heard" the music. I felt his shoulders. I felt the thrill and the joy that was mine because of what he did at the piano; then I felt the piano. And in a week the piano was located.

Now, I will say to anyone – the driver who stole it – if I were now in judgment, I would forgive him. I don't care what motive moved him to do it, I have reached the point: "Forgive him, Father. He knows not what he does." [Luke 23:34]...

But that night, I turned on KPAC, and this lovely piano concerto was coming through, and I used it to aid my imagination and I imagined I was hearing Freedom play that concerto. And I so reveled in the music! It comes on every night between 8:00 and 10:00, that lovely two hours, by the Gas Company; they sponsor it. And here, night after night, if I am home, I turn it on; and I imagined he was doing it. I didn't wait until the person announced who did it. I cut it off before I would be disillusioned in the one playing it. I "heard" Freedom; I imagined that he was doing it. I held him – felt his shoulders, and embraced him and thanked him for the joy I received from the concerto he played.

The next morning at 4:30 his piano is delivered. When he called me the next day to tell me – he has promised to write me, but he is not given to writing; he promised to give me all the details. I know what he is going to do; he is going to wait until he comes down, and then he is going to tell me in the flesh, because he is not given to putting anything down on paper."

Grace Lockwood Roosevelt (7/10/1893 - 6/15/1971) was the wife of Archibald Roosevelt (4/9/1894 - 10/13/1979) who was the fourth child of President Theodore Roosevelt (10/27/1858 - 1/6/1919) and Edith Roosevelt (8/6/1861 - 9/30/1948). In the lecture *Secret Of Imagination* on June 21, 1971 shares two stories about Grace's apartment and her son Archibald Jr. (2/18/1918 - 5/31/1990). Neville said, "I just read a story of a very dear friend of mine who used to come to me – not to my meetings, but I would say once a month she came home for a personal appointment in New York City. She was killed last week in a car driven by her husband. And I can now see this perfectly lovely, gracious lady. She had a home in Oyster Bay, Long Island, and she had her apartment in New York City. Her name is possibly one of the most prominent names in America. The name is Roosevelt. She was of the Teddy Roosevelt branch. Her name was Grace. Her husband was Archibald.

Teddy was Governor of New York; he was Vice President of our Country; he was President of our Country – a very powerful, wonderful leader. He did not leave, as so many presidents leave, a fortune. He didn't go in there to make a fortune. He went in there to lead the country. And he said, "I don't consider public opinion. I perform what I think is best for our country. I feed them what they ought to know. I feed them what I think is best for our country."

But he didn't go in there to make a personal fortune, and he came out without a personal fortune. So she – in spite of her name – did not have a personal fortune. She had a home in Oyster Bay, Long Island, and a lovely apartment – beautifully furnished from things that her father-in-law had given her. If she did not rent her New York apartment for the summer, she could not open her home in Long Island. She could not afford it. Being a lovely home in a very wonderful, fashionable area of New York City, she always got a wonderful price paid in advance for the three or four months. Then came the end of a season where they aren't looking for any homes, and she came to see me.

She said, "Neville, I am desperate. Unless I rent the place in New York City, we can't open our home in Long Island."

> I said, "All right. It's rented, and you are living in Long Island."

"Oh but," she said, "Neville, I can't do that."

I said, "Tonight you sleep in your home in Long Island."

"But," she said, "I can't do that. How could I go and sleep there?"

I said, "You don't do it physically. Tonight you sleep physically in New York City in your apartment, but in your imagination, which is the only reality, you sleep in your home in Long Island, and then you think of your place in New York. The reason why you see it across the East River is because you are physically sleeping in Long Island. And the reason you are sleeping there is because you rented it. Put them all together, that's why you are there."

She said to me, "If it rents, I'll call you."

I said, "There's no if about it. The only if is if you do it. Then you'll call me."

I took her to the elevator. She went downstairs, went back to her place. The next day at 9:00 in the morning Mrs. Roosevelt is on the phone. She said, "Neville, this is Grace Roosevelt."

I said, "How are you, Mrs. Roosevelt?"

She said, "I am calling you from Long Island where I slept last night physically. When I went home, no one came at all over the period that you rent places. But as I got home, soon after I got home, an agent called and asked if I could show the apartment. A single man came in. He liked the place. Money meant nothing to him. He wanted immediate possession, 'but I mean immediate. I mean now!'"

"Well," she said, "I can't get out now. I have to call my husband at the office."

"I don't care what you do. I want immediate possession. And here is my check in advance. You can call the bank to see if the check is good." She got out that day! She called her husband to meet her, and off they went to their home in Long Island.

Well, she was just killed last week, at the age of 73; I think it was. He was driving; he wasn't injured, and the friend in the car was injured, but Grace was killed instantly. But at least, she learned the Law. She didn't come to the meetings very often because she said in her capacity, she was a pillar of the Episcopal Church in New York City – also in Long Island; it would not be advisable to be seen in my meeting place. That would be slumming. But she always came to my home with any problem...

Once she had [a problem] with her son. He came back from Egypt where he was in the State Department, and he came with a huge, big beard, and she said, "Neville, I am embarrassed." It was long before people wore beards; today it would be the thing to do, but he came back long before the young fellows wore beards. It was a huge, big beard. She said, "Neville, I am so embarrassed, I just don't want to walk down Fifth Avenue with him. I would make him walk ahead or walk behind me. I don't want to be seen with him. What must I do? Because he gets annoyed and will do nothing that his father or I suggest."

I said, "How would you feel if you kissed him and he had no beard? You would kiss your son, wouldn't you?"

"Oh, yes."

"Well then, put your hand on his face and he doesn't have any beard, and then kiss him and feel that smooth skin that is your son's face when he has no beard."

"All right, I will do that."

She didn't tell me. I opened the morning paper one Monday-morning. There was a big fashionable social wedding, and here was Mrs. Roosevelt and her husband, and here is her son and here is the bride coming down the steps of the Episcopal Church, and he has no beard! So the next time she came to see me, I reminded her; I said, "You know, you came here the last time about the beard, and the beard is off."

She said, "Do you know why?"

I said, "Yes, I know why, but you tell me why."

"Well, the girl that he married refused to go through with it unless he shaved." She saw the physical fact.

I said, "No, that wasn't it. You promised me that you would kiss him and feel his smooth skin, and if you would feel the smooth skin, it would come off."

She said, "I did do it, but the girl demanded it."

So, she goes back to a physical causation, and it wasn't so at all. There is no natural effect with a natural cause. Every natural effect has an imaginal cause, and the natural only seems. So she still is going to insist that the girl wanted the beard off, and that's why he took it off. Well now, she knows better. She's now in a world just like this. At least she learned the lesson of the Law. She didn't learn the Promise, because when I spoke to her, I did not have the Promise. I had not realized it."

Neville added some more details in the lecture *The Talent* on February 2, 1970 he said, "Now let me tell you the story of a lady I knew in New York City about twenty years ago. I started lecturing on February 2, 1938, sharing my experiences based upon my use of the talent. Shortly after my opening, a lady - very prominent in our country, both politically and socially - began to attend my meetings. She was the daughter-in-law of one who was governor of New York, [later] Vice President, and then President of our country.

One day this lady came to our apartment and told me that she and her husband owned a home in Long Island where they spent their summers, and lease an apartment in New York City where they live during the winter, and always sublet during the summer. Needing the money obtained from renting the apartment to open their home in Long Island, this lady asked for my help.

Although this lady was a pillar of the Episcopal church in New York City and Long Island, she did not go to her ministers, but to me for help. I asked her: "If you sublet your apartment today, where would you sleep tonight?" And she replied, "In Long Island." Then I told her to go home and sleep in Long Island tonight in her imagination. As she is falling asleep, I asked her to think of her New York apartment across the East River and tell herself that she is here in Long Island now because her apartment has been rented. Admitting that, although the idea did not make sense, she [said she] would try it, and promised to call me if it worked. I told her the only "if" to it is "if" she does it!

Two days later this lady called me at 9:00 A.M. from her home in Long Island saying: "Yesterday a gentleman came to see my apartment. He had all the qualifications and money necessary to rent it, but wanted immediate occupancy. I called my husband at the office and that night we physically slept in our home in Long Island." I told her how thrilled I was for her. I had expected her call, but wanted to ask one question: "Did you imagine sleeping in Long Island the night you promised you would?" And she answered: "Yes. I told my husband I was going to retire early as I had an appointment with myself. Then I went to bed assuming I was in Long Island. I thought of my apartment in New York City and felt the relief of knowing it was rented. I took my time looking at the familiar paintings on the walls, the furniture, drapes, and accessories there. Then I fell asleep. The next morning I awoke on my bed in New York City, but because of the series of events which took place that day, we have physically moved to our home in Long Island."

Now, in this lady's mind she is a Christian. She is a gracious, sweet lady, cultured, kind, considerate and generous, but she hasn't the slightest concept as to who Jesus Christ really is. She thinks of him as a man who was born 2,000 years ago, died on a wooden cross, [and] was buried in a grave in the Near East, out of which he rose in some miraculous way. That hasn't a thing to do with Jesus Christ.

Crucified on the cross of your body of flesh and blood, Jesus Christ is your own wonderful human imagination. Buried in your skull, He is dreaming your life into being. Although everything seems so alive here, this world is really His dream of death. But one day He will awaken and you will discover that you are the one spoken of by the prophets and the law of Moses and the Psalms. That there never was another and never will be another...

Another time, this same lady came to me regarding her son, who was in the State Department in the Near East. Long before hippies came into being, her son wore a beard. She wanted him to shave it off, so I suggested that she kiss him and feel the smooth skin on his cheek and chin. This she promised to do.

One morning I opened the New York Times to the Social page where I saw a picture of her son without a beard. The next time this lady came to see me I mentioned seeing her son clean shaven and she said: "I imagined kissing him and feeling his face, but because he fell in love with a girl in the State Department who didn't like his beard, he shaved it off." She attributed the shaving of the beard to the means rather than the cause, which was what she had done in her imagination. The girl was only the instrument which brought it about. Having forgotten when she planted the seed, this lady didn't recognize her own harvest."

Joseph Berlay (circa 1894 - 4/9/1971) was married to Louise Berlay who was a student of Neville's and wrote the book called *Magic Of The Mind*. In the lecture *The Artist Is God* on May 19, 1969 Neville said, "Let me share with you a simple story. A very dear friend of mine who lives in New York City was born in Russia of a very poor Jewish family. He knew what it was like to be frightened when he heard the Cossacks were coming, for they burned homes and caused pain for the sheer joy of frightening people. Joseph was the eldest of a family of five, a boy not more than nine or ten when his mother died, leaving his father to maintain his family alone. Little Joseph found a job taking money from a store to the bank and having it changed into smaller denominations. He had never known what it was like to wear shoes, but wrapped his feet in newspapers or whatever he could find to keep them warm. His clothes had always come from charity, but he - like all men - brought his innate knowledge with him when he came into this world.

So, one day, as he watched the cashier changing the money he brought, he noticed that the big copper coins, when rolled in paper, resembled the silver coins, even though their value was widely separated. Then he said to himself: "Wouldn't it be wonderful if he made a mistake?" and in his imagination Joseph took the money rolled through the window to him in the assumption that the mistake was already made. He then walked back to the shop, filled with the sense of joy. Reason told him no mistake was made, but he thought of all the things he could buy if he had the money. He would buy a pair of slacks, a pair of shoes, and eat until it came out of his ears - a thing he had never experienced before. He had the satisfaction of walking those many blocks in the mood of having what he wanted.

The next day, when Joseph returned to the same teller, the man made the mistake. As Joseph left the bank he wrestled with himself, but his poverty and embarrassment were greater than his ethical code; so he went to another bank and changed the money into the correct denominations and kept the overage. That night he bought himself a pair of slacks, new shoes, and ate at a restaurant until he could eat no more. He told me that although he wrestled with his conscience all night, he could not justify his act; but he learned a lesson. He learned that Sir Anthony Eden was right when he said: "An assumption, though false, if persisted in will harden into fact."

Sir Anthony did not need position or money, but he knew a law which undoubtedly he used through his years. Today my friend Joseph is a multi-millionaire. I am quite sure he is far, far richer in Caesar's dollars and cents than Anthony Eden, for Joseph learned and lived by this knowledge. He never duns his customers. When they are long overdue in payment, Joseph sits alone and mentally writes a letter thanking the man for the receipt of his check - and within four days he receives it. If poverty would teach this lesson to everyone, all should be born equally poor. Joseph now lives in an apartment in New York City where he pays $12,000 a year in rent as well as $45,000 a year rent for his street business. He now has businesses in Paris, Puerto Rico, and Brazil, for he learned how to move. Leaving Russia at the age of sixteen, Joseph found a job driving a garbage truck in France, where - seemingly by accident - he met the great dancer, Anna Pavlova. She suggested he follow in his father's footsteps and make undergarments for women, which he did and is now famous for.

I am asking you to do as Joseph did, for I am teaching you a principle, and leave you to your choice and its risk. I have told this story in the past and there has always been someone in the audience who has criticized me for telling it, claiming I am leading people astray. I have always had a suspicion, however, that those who are most vocal in their criticism are justifying their own behavior. I am not urging you to forget all these so-called codes, but to tell you that we all ate of the tree of good and evil, and have suffered ever since. I am not suggesting you go out and steal from anyone, or that Joseph should - as some have suggested - pay the money back. If he did, to whom would he send it, to Stalin? Well, Stalin stole the entire country, not just a few coins as Joseph did. No, Joseph has given tens of thousands of dollars to help friends and charities, not to justify his act as a child, but out of the goodness of his heart"

On April 23, 1971 in the lecture *Consigned To Disobedience* Neville added, "Here is a simple story . A boy born in poverty, born in Odessa, Russia, in a Jewish family who knew nothing of full meals; he was the oldest of a family of five. At a very tender age his mother died, leaving just a few babies. He was then maybe, I would say, ten. He had to work to support the family. His father was a worker, but could not bring in enough to feed the family. He never knew what it was to have a new pair of shoes, a new pair of pants, a new shirt, a new hat. Everything was given by charity, and these gifts were not new things;they were simply hand-me-downs, what people had on. So, when he wore out the burlap shoe, he could go back and get another pair of things to wrap his foot in cold Russia.

He got a job going to the bank every day with large denominations of paper, and they would be exchanged for silver and copper. So when he came back he had the equal amount of money, this time in silver and copper. And one day, standing before the teller, the cashier, he noticed that the copper and the silver had similar external markings; they looked alike. And he wondered to himself, "wouldn't it be wonderful if he made a mistake? Wouldn't it be wonderful if that cashier made a mistake and gave me silver instead of copper?"

At that moment he assumed that the cashier did, and in his mind's eye he took the things and then walked back to the store. He knew the cashier had not done it, but he simply wiped it out and played a little game. And he walked back feeling that the cashier had made the mistake and he wondered: "Now what would I do? I will go into a restaurant and eat for the first time in my life to where I feel satisfied. I will eat until it comes through my ears, then I'll buy a pair of shoes and then I'll buy a pair of slacks." He knew that it would cover that much. When he got back to the store the man hadn't made a mistake, but he had the joy of walking in that assumption.

The next day the man made that mistake. And he realized it the minute the man made the mistake. So he went to another bank and changed the money into the right amount so that he could take back the right amount to the store, leaving this money over. And with that extra money, he said, "I wrestled all day with myself, and that night when I went to bed I could hardly sleep. I wrestled and wrestled with myself because that was in conflict with what my dead mother had taught me. 'Thou shalt not steal, thou shalt not covet.' The next day my hunger and my desire to have a new pair of shoes and a new pair of pants overpowered what I had heard from my mother, and I ate until it came through, not my ears, but till I was stuffed. Then I bought myself a pair of slacks and I bought myself a pair of shoes."...

So you find yourself, as he did, hungry and embarrassed because of the rags that he wore; and he learned that the Law is spiritual. So he rose from the state as a little, impoverished, Jewish boy in Odessa, in Russia. And after the revolution he found himself, when the war came to an end, among soldiers who left Russia and made their way to France. So when he died at the age of 77 on Good Friday,—this past Good Friday—he could leave an estate that runs into millions. He learned the Law.

He learned that the Law is spiritual. And he told me himself he never took a man to court for unpaid bills. He would sit at his desk when all the employees left and he would write out a letter thanking the man for his check. He never mailed it, but he would get himself into that mood and thank them for the check that they had sent. And he said, "Within a matter of days, never in excess of a week, but quite often two or three days, a check came." The check came to him in payment of an unpaid bill that was long overdue. "But," he said, "I never once had to lose a friend, for I cannot remain in business and lose customers; so I never had to dun a customer. I've learned the Law. I learned that these assumptions, though denied by my senses, if I really believe them and put all my faith in the assumption, it would become a reality. And so, I lived by it. Long before I met you Neville,—long before I ever heard of you. I heard of you only through my wife. She heard of you and heard the Law, and we sort of struck it off together when we were in Paris; but long before I met her or met you, I proved this law when I was a poor little boy in Russian, and I began to live by it. So I have never once taken a man to court to get back monies I had advanced in the form of merchandise."

So when he died at the ripe old age of 77,—he died quite suddenly of a heart attack,—well, he had proven that Paul's words were right; and he didn't know Paul, for he was born and raised in the Jewish faith; and I doubt that he ever read the New Testament. So when Paul makes the statement in the 7th chapter of Romans that: "The Law is spiritual,"—when he makes that bold statement that: "If it were not for the Law, I never should have known sin. I should not have known what it is to covet if the Law had not said, 'You shall not covet.' So, God has consigned all men to disobedience, that He may have mercy on all.'"

Ray Lee was an ad man who was very successful using the Law and Neville would share Ray's stories. On July 18, 1968 in the lecture *Prophetic Sketches* Neville said, "Here is a friend of mine in L.A. He comes to all the meetings, a handsome, wonderful lad of about 40 years of age. He says, "In my office this perfectly lovely girl, she serves all the different gentlemen who are in the office and we all love her. One day she came into my office, and she spent twenty minutes telling me of the horrors of this world, where there are so few eligible men for marriage, and so many jerks – millions of jerks and so few eligible men. So, after she poured it out for twenty minutes, I didn't say a word to her; she left the office, and I sat there for a few minutes, and I heard within me – I heard her tell me that she had met the man – the most glorious man that ever walked this earth, and they are dating and – oh, she's just walking in the heavens. I did it at that moment. On my way home, driving on the freeway, I did it again. The next morning when I was shaving, I thought of her, and I did it again. Well, in ten days I had no confirmation of it. She still came into the office bringing the papers; and as she came in and she still seemed to be gloomy, I did it again. Well, ten days went by, and all of a sudden she came in, and here is sheer ecstasy! She spent one-half hour of my precious time telling me of the man of men in this world. They are dating, and they are dating night after night. Why, there's not a person in this world comparable to this man."

Well, what did he do? He simply used his imagination to give her what she wanted. She wanted a man, not a jerk; so he simply got a man. And, now, as far as she is concerned, he is just the best man in this world. Well, I closed on this very last Friday in June; so I do not know if it is consummated or not – I don't know. But they are dating every, every day; and as far as she is concerned he is the only man in the world. But who did it? My friend, his name is Ray Lee. He sat down – he likes her as a friend, and all the men in the office – they like her. She has worked in the office for a while. It's an advertising office. And Ray, knowing this principle, he figures, "All right, we'll forget all of the people in this world that she thinks are no good, and I will now see that she has a perfect man." And that's all that Ray did. On his way home, he did it; next morning when he was shaving, he did it; and he was reminded by her gloom that something must be done more than what he did, so he did it again. So, he did it maybe four or five times in that interval; and in less than two weeks, she finds an angel on earth. Of course, he may not always be that; but, nevertheless, at the moment, he is all that he (Ray Lee) wanted her to find.

You can have anything in this world – I don't care what it is, if you'll apply God's law. And God's law is simple: Whatever you desire, believe that you have received it, and you will. Well, if you believe that you've received it how would you feel? Just how would you feel? That's the feeling – catch it! Catch that feeling, and don't let it go! You have found Me; well, don't let Me go. Let all the others go, but don't let Me go. You have found salvation in that mood. That mood, were it true, would save you from all that you formerly had but you didn't want."

In the lecture *Walk On The Water* on June 20, 1968 he said, "Let me now share some experiences of a friend who practices the art of walking on the water. In his letter he said: "There is a lady in my office who was constantly talking about the absence of decent, eligible men in her life, claiming they were all riffraff and no good. Six weeks ago, while driving home from work, I revised her words. I heard her tell me she was dating a marvelous man and sharing the wonderful things they were doing. Recently this lady was so glum, I reminded myself to revise her words again, so I did. Yesterday she spent twenty minutes telling me of the perfect gentleman she is now dating. He must be terrific, for this lady is now walking in ecstasy."

Then he continued, saying: "An associate asked me to write a news review for his client. I gathered all of the material together that I would need, put it in a folder and placed it on my desk, which was piled high with pending work. Then one Friday my associate said: 'My client wants to see me next Monday at 9:00 A.M. in his office,' and I realized that I must produce the news review at that time. Immediately I sat down and imagined it was 5:00 P.M. My review was completed, read by my associate, and approved. I heard him say: 'It is just fine.' Satisfied with that scene as my end result, I found the folder, sat down at my typewriter and typed four pages, as everything flowed smoothly. At 5:00 that afternoon my associate stopped by my office, read the report, and said the exact words I had heard him say in my imagination: 'It is just fine.'"

Neville shared a story by Ray about his friend worried that he was going to be fired. In the lecture *All Things Exist* on May 24, 1968 Neville said, "A friend recently wrote saying: "Three weeks ago a friend called, saying he was afraid he was going to be fired. I instantly revised his call. Hearing his voice bubbling with excitement, he told me how he had been praised for his work and I felt the thrill of rejoicing with him. Today he came to my office and said the very words I heard in my imagination. "This morning, while dressing I was thinking about an ad I was working on which carried the name of a very prominent man in San Francisco. As I ran the ad through my mind I said to myself, I want to put the word 'Mister' before his name. I did it and it felt right. I made a mental note to do it when I arrived at the office, and promptly dropped the thought. That afternoon the man called, asking that I insert 'Mister' before his name - not in the ad, but in a radio commercial where his name was used. "Then my friend added this thought: "I stand in awe at the operation of this law. You asked about the little pig I saw. He was small, but fat, and the way I am stuffing him today, in no time at all he will be so large he will fill this room. For those who are not familiar with this symbol, the pig is the symbol of Christ, the power and wisdom of God. Every time you exercise your imagination lovingly on behalf of another or yourself, you are feeding Jesus Christ. My friend is stuffing his pig, because every moment of time he is alert and putting this law into practice."

Ray's story about creating a 75 million profit for his clients. On July 23, 1968 in the lecture *Power* Neville said, "This man has a terrific control of this power. He is an advertising agent. About, I would say, in the early part of this year, his boss said to him, "This is our best account, and I don't want to lose it. But you know the industry today. It's on the skids, and we must do something to pull it out." Well, he sat down and said "If imagining creates reality, my only problem will be to face these men who believe themselves so wise, and persuade them to let me go all out with my campaign from the premise that it is already an accomplished fact. I can't advertise that this thing is possible. I've got to say it has been tried and proven in my ads." He worked out the entire thing.

When these twenty men, all multi-millionaires (for this is one of the huge industries of the world, this is an international industry) – when he worked the entire thing out and presented it to these twenty men on the board, they thought themselves above all this. They were ethically above all things. Their moral code would not allow it, but my friend persuaded them that this is how the law operates, that imagining creates reality. "So if you want something created, leave it to me. I will take your desire and make it something that is already a fact. You voice it." The first quarter of this year that industry not only arrested the motion downward, but turned it around, and their profits – not their gross – their profits for the first quarter of this year were seventy-five million dollars more than the first quarter of last year – seventy-five million more. I am speaking of a net profit. Now these wise men, with their wonderful ethical codes – they allow it! They saw the money in the bank. They saw all these things, and their so-called ethical moral code went through the window because they saw another principle, which they did not know.

His competitor (I saw the letter) – his competitor in the advertising field wrote the boss, my friend's boss. He said, "You know, I take my hat off to you. You use a principle that we have always used in our work," (which was a darned lie; he never did it at all). He said, "I know exactly what you did." He's trying to fish him out to find out what he is doing, and in this letter he makes the claim that he actually knew and had always used it, "And no one can work for our concern unless he is aware of this principle and lives by it. We aren't concerned about his religious background. He may be a Catholic, Protestant, Jew, or an atheist, but he has to live by this principle." Well, I saw that letter. The man was fishing, just fishing to get the one who really conceived it to come forward and tell him what he did…

And this one, in his advertising agency, he can write his own ticket today. The boss said to him, "What do you want?" The boss gives him – well, I would say three or four times a year – a huge big unsolicited bonus check. He wants to keep him. My friend has no desire to quit, but the boss is so eager to hold him, he gets one bonus after the other. And my friend? All right, he'll take it. Why shouldn't he? "

Ray's story about seeing his friend employed with a 25% increase in pay after his employer said they were considering letting him go. In the lecture *Live In The End* on July 19, 1968 Neville said, "Here is a friend of mine in L.A., and this man was unmercifully bawled out by his supervisors, and told that he was no earthly good, and they are considering letting him go. They are going to fire him. Well, the man had no support outside of the job, and he had a family. He told my friend. Well, my friend lives by this law, so he said to him, "All right, go your way." He didn't tell him what he was going to do.

He sat quietly at his desk and heard the man tell him that they praised him beyond measure for something that he had done. It wasn't 48 hours that they had a complete reversal of their attitude towards this man in their praise for something he did in the advertising world. But the blow left its mark, and he said to my friend, "Yes, they've reversed it, but I don't feel easy on the job, because they could not have said the unlovely things that they said and forgotten them, so it will come back, and I'm going to quit. I have no money. I'm giving them two weeks' notice. I am going to ask them to give me one week of the two, that I can get myself together and maybe take off a few days and just get my thoughts in order."

Well, at the end of two weeks he didn't have a job. My friend – when he told him what he was going to do – my friend knew he could not afford to quit and not work, so he saw him gainfully employed and earning twenty-five percent more than the present job. He took off the second week. When he came back at the end of the first week, he came into my friend's office and said, "Only yesterday I got the offer, and I start Monday. I do not lose one day's salary, and I start at twenty five per cent more than I received on the past job.

What did it? My friend's imagination, a loving use of the imagination on behalf of a friend! Had he gone without that imaginal state, he would have walked into the place, and the man would have said, "We have nothing," or, "We can't use you," "Why are you quitting?" He didn't ask anything; he simply wanted the man.

So, if you precede your visit by an imaginal act, they will see you as you see yourself. If you walk in knowing that you're no good, they will see you exactly that way. But if you walk in the assumption that things are as you desire them to be, they are going to see you that way. And this is life."

On July 16, 1969 in the lecture *Many Mansions* Neville shared two stories of a friend named Dick. He said, 'Let me share with you an experience of just a few months ago. This friend of mine – a very marvelous chap – an executive in a very prominent advertising agency in Los Angeles (he comes to all the meetings). Here are two short ones: He said, "I was driving home, and then it dawned upon me: You know that April the fifteenth is just around the corner, and you could do with some cash for Uncle Sam." Now, he receives a very large salary, but he spends it and he lives a lovely, generous life. He has a lovely home and three children. He maintains a beautiful home, but he never thought in terms of these moments in time when we are confronted with Uncle Sam's outstretched hand and he wants a part of what you earn. Well, you can't say "No" to him; you've got to pay him. So here comes around the corner the fifteenth of April, and he could use some cash.

"Riding home," he said, "this is what I did. I simply imagined, and I made a game of it. I imagined that it was raining gently, but the rain was little green pieces of paper. It was money coming gently upon me, and I could feel it – actually feel the gentle rain of paper money dropping upon me, and I had stopped. I had done this for about two or three minutes, [and] then the traffic demanded all of my attention and so I broke it. When I went home that night I thought it was great fun and I'd try it again. I could feel it actually descending upon me like a gentle rain. The next day was the fourteenth of April, and sitting at my desk (not paying any attention to it, really) the boss comes in, and he said to me: 'You have a ten per cent raise and it's retroactive as of the first of the month,' and gave me a check for a ten per cent raise." And he makes a very big salary. So, ten percent of a very large salary, and it was retroactive to the first of the month – here, within a matter of moments, his feeling was granted as an actual fact! He didn't have it before he started, and now he has it. The vision came to flower at the appointed hour. He needed it on the fifteenth and here, just before the fifteenth, a man comes through with a check and tells him that it is retroactive to the first, at ten per cent beyond what he got last month.

Now, this is a story that I have at home (at the hotel) in his own hand. He didn't confine me to some secrecy. He told it to me – not in confidence, but that I may share it with others to encourage them to try it. "Now," he said, "I went home a couple of months before, and my wife began to tell me a very unlovely story – unlovely in the sense that we love the little girl. She's fourteen months old, and we know her grandmother well. Of course we know the mother, but we are closer to the grandmother, and the grandmother told my wife that the little girl began to develop bumps in her neck – little swellings. So they took her to the hospital for observation. They made a biopsy and five doctors brought in the negative verdict that it was malignant; it was cancer." Well, in a child of fourteen months that is fatal, because you are developing. You can arrest cancer if you are my age because you are not building any more – and they drop from this world by some other means – because at my age if I was told I had cancer, it doesn't mean that that will be the cause of my future departure from this world. For I am not building any longer; I am just holding my own. Well, a little child of fourteen months builds rapidly, so whatever is in her is building rapidly. With cancer, in no time they are gone. So the grandmother was scared; the mother was scared.

But as his wife was telling my friend, he said: "I allowed her voice to tell me completely different. I heard just enough. She kept on talking, but she didn't know from my expression that I wasn't listening. I didn't hear one word after I heard what she said, and as she kept on building the picture, her voice faded from me. And then I reconstructed what she said, and I had her tell me that the whole thing was false. Although there were five doctors, each agreeing that this thing was malignant and therefore fatal, I let it fade completely and brought in a complete reversal of that verdict."

Now the grandmother asked that they keep the child a little longer at the hospital that they could still bring in another. So, they made another biopsy from a different section of the neck. A sixth doctor was brought in. "I am sorry to disagree with my men in the profession, but it is not malignant and it is not cancer." They then were called in to make a third, and they confessed that they were wrong because she couldn't possibly have had cancer and today not have cancer. So they had to justify it. They could not for one moment; they confessed they were wrong. He said: "That's all right with me. The child now lives and she has no cancer. Why should I go out and tell them: No, they were right in the first time, but prayer to the only God that exists can make all things possible? With God, all things are possible, but you don't know who God is, so you believe in your technique. It's perfectly all right."

He said: "Now, my wife told me exactly what I knew." The grandmother is now telling it all over the neighborhood, and now they look upon me as a miracle man – which is unfortunate, because it will make life difficult for me in the neighborhood." He said: "I'm no miracle man; I simply learned through you who God is. And if all things are possible to God, and God is my own Imagination, can't I imagine what I want to imagine and persuade myself of the reality of the state imagined? Well, I did, and the child now is free of what they called cancer. But to justify their own decision and not say: 'Well, we were wrong,' they now say it could not have been cancer or therefore she could not have overcome it."

So, here is that story I've just told you, plus the raise in salary, and unnumbered things the man lives by. He is not interested in the

Promise. Well that's all right. He's a businessman, and he has to pay rent, buy clothes for his children and his wife and himself. And he's more interested in the Law, and so he's always writing these stories concerning the Law. If, perchance, I get off and week after week, I'm stressing the Promise, I can see Dick – that night he isn't going to come. Well, it doesn't interest him but it's perfectly all right, because we're living in the world of Caesar, and we've got to master this Law and not pass the buck and blame others for the things that are happening in our world, for in my Father's house are unnumbered mansions. It sets me now on my feet to become discriminating, to become selective. Into what mansion will I go this night? Into what state of consciousness will I go this night? For, if I occupy it, even though I forget it tomorrow, it will not be forgotten. I have planted the seed, and in time – and on time – it will come up as a harvest. Whether I recognize my own planting or not, it's coming into my world. So, why not devote some time every day to planting lovely things in this world?...

So, he's riding home in his car and money is falling on him – gently falling, green money – and then in a matter of moments he gets a raise. Why did that man have the impulse to give him a ten per cent raise? Because he appropriated it. You can work for a firm, as you know, all your life and it would never occur to the boss to give you a raise. And going in and begging him for it isn't going to do it. You've got to appropriate it first, and then let him think that he initiated it and give it to you"

In the lecture *Power Called "The Law"* on April 21, 1969 Neville said, "Let me share with you now a couple of stories a gentleman shared with me this week. He said: "About ten days ago my wife told me of a little girl only fourteen months old who had developed lumps on her neck [in] which - when the doctor removed and tested a lump - there were signs of cancer. Three specialists had been brought in and each separately had declared the child had cancer. Only one doctor, looking at the results, questioned the verdict, but they were keeping the child in the hospital for further examination. As I listened to her story I cued my wife's voice out to the point that I couldn't even hear what she was saying, but hearing her voice, I reconstructed the story and heard its revision in my minds eye. That night as I fell asleep I listened again and heard my wife tell me the revised story. A few days later the doctors made another test from another lump and the vote was unanimous, the child did not have cancer. And since they had performed no remedial treatment in the hospital, they determined she never did have cancer, for without treatment the child could not have overcome the condition. When my wife heard the new verdict she told the grandmother and the mother what I had done, but they could not believe that an imaginal act has any power of causation."

To the world it is the height of insanity to believe that imagining creates reality, yet every mystic knows that every natural effect has a spiritual cause. A natural cause only seems to be. It is a delusion of this world, as man's memory is so poor he cannot relate what is taking place now to a former imaginal act. Always looking for physical causation, man cannot believe he imagined anything that could have produced such a physical effect; yet I tell you: as you sit alone and imagine you are setting a cause in motion, and when you see its effects you may deny the imaginal state, but your "now" is alive and real to you because of an imaginal act on your part and for no other reason. Your imagination sets everything in motion, but your memory is faulty; therefore you may look upon one who claims life is caused by imagination as a fool - yet Blake would call you an idiot reasoner, not a man of imagination. Now, my friend continued, saying: "Driving home from work the other night I was thinking I could use a little more cash, as Uncle Sam would be making demands upon my income. Then I began to imagine lovely, green, crisp currency raining down on me. For about one minute I lost myself in a little shower of green currency. Then the traffic demanded my attention and I assumed my normal, alert state and forgot all about my imaginal act until the morning of the fifteenth of April. At that time my boss entered the office and said: 'You will receive a ten per cent raise in salary retroactive to April first,' and handed me a check."

Now, let me warn you tonight, wait until you get home to try it. It's much better to imagine the crisp currency falling on your bed than on the freeway! But do it, for I tell you everything is an imaginal act. There is no such thing as physical causation. It's all imaginal, but the world will not accept it. They laugh at the man of imagination but they cannot disprove it. A man may physically strike another. That was the physical cause while the blow he received was the effect; therefore the whole thing appeared to be constructed physically, but I ask you: what preceded the impulse to strike? That impulse was the unseen cause, which was an imaginal act. The world is brought into being by imagination and sustained by imagination, and when imagination no longer sustains it, it dissolves and leaves not a trace behind. One must approach the gospel on this level first. If one's interest is aroused on this level and it is proved to be true in the testing, then they may be interested in hearing about the promise.

Now I go back to the little girl. Judged by human standards the garment she wears is only fourteen months old, but the wearer of that garment is as old as God himself, and God has no beginning and no end. He chose us in him, not when we came out from our mother's womb, but before the foundation of the world. Before physical creation you and I were chosen in him for a purpose, for without purpose what would anything matter if death was final?...

My friend knows nothing about cancer. If he saw a cancer cell under a microscope he wouldn't recognize it. He is not a doctor and knows no more about the human body than I do, but he does know what his wife would tell him if the verdict was reversed and the child was well. When his wife told her friend of her husband's imaginal act, the friend (as the world) dismissed the idea, for she could not believe that causation was mental. To her everything has a physical cause and must be cured physically, yet I tell you: life itself is an imaginal journey.

My friend heard his wife tell him of the child and then, knowing what he wanted to hear, he changed her words in his imagination. That is all he did. And those words could not return unto him void, but had to accomplish that which he purposed on the inside. He did nothing on the outside to bring it to pass. He simply remained faithful to his imaginal act and it was fulfilled."

Neville talked about his friend Benny Gould in the lecture *Awake O Sleeper* on July 25, 1968 he said, "This friend of mine down south, Benny Gould –a friend called him and said, "You know, our little daughter, six months old – the doctor says she will not live the week; that she now has meningitis, and the crisis is now."

My friend Benny, instead of sympathizing with this father – he bawled him out. He said, "Didn't you tell me that you are a good Christian? You go to your Baptist church, and you consider yourself a good Christian? I don't go to the Baptist Church. In fact, I don't go to church, but I consider myself a good Christian. What are you doing accepting the verdict of the doctor? Why can't you now accept the teaching of Scripture and believe in your heart that the little girl that I saw a matter of moments after she was born is now alive and thriving?"

After he bawled his friend out, Benny put the receiver up and then sat down and heard that man's voice, as though he called him on the telephone; and then he heard the man tell him that the child has miraculously recovered. That's all that Benny did.

That night a lady had a dream, and because it was related to Benny, she called Benny the next day and told Benny the dream, and this was the dream. She said, "I had a strange dream last night, Benny. I dreamt I was in a hospital, in the lobby, and two nurses were discussing a certain case of a friend of yours, a little girl, and one said to the other, 'But who paid for the operation? Who paid the expense of the hospital?' And one nurse said to the other, 'Benny did.'"

That was only a dream. Well, Benny did pay for it – not in dollars and cents, he said the price. The price was that he represented the father to himself in a different way altogether, not complaining, not feeling sorry, not feeling sad at heart, but he heard that man's voice with a joy in it telling him that the little girl had recovered miraculously. That's all that Benny did. Well, that's paying the price...

Benny simply put the receiver down, brought his mind upon the same voice, but changed the conversation. And it was confirmed in the not-distant future. That entire thing changed in the outer world to conform to what Benny had done in the inner world, all in his imagination."

In the lecture *Yours For The Taking* on September 18, 1967 Neville shared some of Benny's experiences. Neville said, "Now, let me share with you three stories which came to me during the summer. The first letter was from my friend Benny. In it he told of lying prone on his bed, face down, when he felt as though someone grabbed his shoulders; and as he was lifted up he heard the words: "Take a stand!" Intuitively he knew he had to make the decision now as to whether he was going to believe that imagining creates reality or disbelieve it.

Scripture tells us, "He who is not with me is against me." There is no neutral ground, for "I have not come to bring peace, but a sword. To set a man against his father and a daughter against her mother." Why? Because a man's enemies are within him. Everyone must eventually take the stand that imagining creates reality and swim or sink with this concept.

Now, a few days later while in meditation, Benny felt himself being held from behind by three men. As they raised him, he watched the sun rise and heard the words: "Look! Behold!" and "Recognition!" And he remembered a passage from my book, Your Faith Is Your Fortune: "Recognition of this truth will transform you from one who tries to make it so, into one who recognizes it to be so."

Soon after this, a friend asked Ben to pray for him. He wanted to be the property manager of the company he worked for. Although he had been passed by year after year, Benny told him what to do, and imagined hearing the friend tell him the job was now his. A few months later the job was vacated and his friend was given the position with an increase in salary and greater responsibility, just as he had imagined. What did Benny do? He imagined! To whom did he pray? To his own wonderful human imagination! God, the creator of all life, is like pure imagining in you, underlying all of your faculties - including perception. He streams into your surface mind least disguised in the form of productive fantasy. Benny took a stand. He prayed for his friend and believed his prayer was answered. He tested himself, and the windows of heaven opened and poured forth blessings for all to see. Now Benny knows that with God all things are possible."

Neville shared a story about Jimmy Fuller and also talked about Abdullah. In the 1953 lecture *Changing The Feeling Of "I"* he said, "Now, let me tell you a story. A few years ago in this city I was giving a series of lectures down near that lake - I can't even recall the name of the lake but it was some Parkview Manor was the place where I spoke, and in that audience was a gentleman who sought an audience before the meeting. And we went across the street into the little park there, and he said to me that he had an insoluble problem. I said, "There is no such thing as an insoluble problem. "But", he said, "you do not know my problem. It's not a state of health, I assure you; it is, look at the skin that I wear". I said, "What's wrong with it; it looks lovely to me". He said, "Look at the pigment of my skin. I, by the accident of birth, am now discriminated against. The opportunities for progress in this world are denied me just because of the accident of birth, that I was born a colored man. Opportunities for advancement in every field, neighborhoods that I would like to live in and raise a family I couldn't move in, where I would like to open up a business I couldn't move into that area."

Then I told him my own personal experience, that I came to this country. Well, I didn't have that problem but I was a foreigner in the midst of all Americans. I didn't find it difficult. "Yet", as he reminded me, "but that's not my problem, Neville. Others have come here speaking with an accent, but they haven't my skin, and I was born an American". Then I told him an experience of mine in New York City. If I were called upon to name a man that I would consider my teacher, I would name Abdullah. I studied with that gentleman for five years. He had the same color skin, the same pigment as this gentleman. He would never allow anyone to refer to him as a colored man. He was very proud of being a negro didn't want any modification of what God had made him. He turned to me and he said, "Have you ever seen a picture of the Sphinx?"

I said, "Yes".

He said, "It embodies the four fixed quarters of the universe. You have the lion, the eagle, the bull, and man. And here is man that is the head. The crown of that creature called the Sphinx, which still defies man's knowledge to unriddle it, was crowned with a human head. And look carefully at the head, Neville, and you will see whoever modeled that head must have been a negro. Whoever modeled it had the face of a negro and if that still defies man's ability to unravel it, I am very proud that I am a negro."

I have seen scientists, doctors, lawyers, bankers, from every walk of life seek an audience with old Abdullah, and everyone Who came thought themselves honored to be admitted to his home and to receive an interview. If he was ever invited out, and he was, he was always the honored guest.

He said, "Neville, you must first start with self. Find self, don't be ashamed ever of the being you are. Discover it and start the changing of that self".

Well, I told this gentleman exactly what Abdullah had taught me, that there was no cause outside of the arrangement of his own mind. If he was discriminated against, it was not because of the pigment of his skin, though he showed me signs as large as all outdoors denying him access to a certain area. The sign is there only because in the minds of some men such patterns are formed and they draw unto themselves what now they would condemn; that there is no power outside the mind of man to do anything to man, and he by the arrangement of his own mind, by consenting to these restrictions in his cradle and being conditioned slowly through his youth, waking into manhood believing himself set upon would have to be set upon, but "no man cometh unto me save I call him".

So then someone comes to condemn or to praise. They couldn't come unless I call them. Not a man called Neville, but that secret being that is not called Neville. The secret being that is the sum total of all of my beliefs, all of the things that I consent to, that form a pattern of structure, that secret being draws unto itself things in harmony with itself. Well, that man went away and wrestled with himself. He couldn't believe everything I told him, not that night, but last Sunday morning in the lobby, he came forward and we renewed the friendship. He took me next door to show me the fruit of this teaching.

He said, "Neville, it took me almost three years to really overcome that fixed idea that I, by the accident of birth, would be a secondary citizen, but I overcame it. Now here is my office on Wilshire Boulevard. I picked this one not because it was the only one offered; four equally wonderful spots were offered me. I took this one because it had greater telephone facilities , but the others were equally good. Now here is my office.Now you couldn't judge my income from this office, lovely as it is. Everything is nice about it, but, Neville,this year I will net a quarter of a million dollars". Well in America that is still a fabulous sum of money. It would be staggering in any other part of the world, but even in fabulous America a man to net a quarter of a million is really up in the very highest of brackets. And that was the man that a few years ago told me the whole vast world was against him by reason of the accident of birth. He knows now he is what he is by virtue of the state of consciousness with which he is identified, and the choice is his to go back to the restrictions of his childhood when he believed the story or to continue in the freedom that he has found...

So I told this story at a small gathering here in the city, and not very many asked questions about it, but three people asked, "But he must have had money before. He must have known the right people. He must in some way have had some substance to start it, because how can you go out to loan a hundred million dollars and call that a real fact of being that you have that to loan and tell me you didn't have someone who had it or you, yourself, didn't have it". I did not ask the gentleman about the individual facts of the case. I went into the office, I saw it, I didn't look at his books; he volunteered this information, and gave me the figure of a quarter of a million net for the year. I have not checked or in any way verified the statement; I believe it implicitly. But I will not go along with those who believe that unless you have certain things to start with you can't apply this law.

You can start now from scratch and choose the being you want to be. You aren't going to change the pigment of your skin but you will find your accent or the pigment of skin or your so-called racial background will not be a hindrance, for if a man is ever hindered it can only be the state of consciousness in which he abides that hinders him. Man is freed or constrained by reason of the state of mind in which he persists. If you persist in it, well, then I will say, "persist in it", but I warn you no one cares and that is an awful blow when a man discovers that no one, no one but himself really cares. So we find ourselves weeping with ourselves in the hope of getting others to weep with us. And what an awful shock when the day arrives we discover that no one really ever cared. They will give us some little listening ear for a moment just as they were passing by, but they really didn't care."

In the 1953 lecture *Sound Investments* Neville talked about Jimmie's many success stories. He said, "Now I told a story here two weeks ago of Jimmie Fuller. Well, I didn't have all the details of the story, but after the meeting; dozens of you said to me, not only after the meeting that day, but after my meetings at the Ebell Theatre, that Jimmie Fuller, to have made the fortune that he made, must have had great capital. Well, I could neither affirm nor deny your bold assertion, for you spoke as though you knew and many of you almost convinced me that he had great capital and that's why he turned it into great returns. So on Friday night I asked him to tell me more of the details. He said "When you came here four years ago, Neville, I came to hear you. My wife asked me 'Why do you come to hear Neville? Who told you of Neville? He said, I turned the radio on one night and I heard Dr. Bailes. I had never heard of the man before. At the end of his lecture, which I thoroughly enjoyed, he said Neville is coming to speak for us and it's a MUST. Well the next night, I so liked Dr. Bailes that I turned him on the next night, and for the next two weeks he kept on promoting you, and he was so generous in his praise, I thought I've got to hear this man. So when I came, I enjoyed what I heard on Sunday morning, and then you announced you were speaking the following night at this place, but it was two dollars. Well, he said, between myself and the next I actually had Fifty four dollars. I had a wife and a little boy; we couldn't leave the little child alone; he was a babe: it meant a sitter-in, but my wife and I came to everything you gave and one night we could not pay the sitter-in; we just didn't have it, but we took our last which was fifty four dollars and came to your every meeting - the two of us - and one night we didn't have it to pay that sitter-in. Three years later, Neville, I had not proven your theory. You know my problem, as I told you before."

Perchance there is someone here who did not hear it - the man is a negro, and his problem was that because he was a negro, all the marks and stripes of the world were against him. I tried to convince him it was only in his own mind that these stripes were placed; his acceptance of that as restriction made it restriction, but if he could only drop it by non-acceptance, by complete indifference, to the pigment of skin he could accomplish his every dream by acceptance of it now.

Well, in the last year, Jimmie Fuller by complete acceptance, investing his moment, his now, has turned the year into a net profit of two hundred and fifty thousand dollars. He did not have one penny when he started; he did not raise large capital; he didn't have it. He only invested God's coin. God gave it to him. He gave him the moment, which is time. So instead of spending his thought, which everyone has, and spending his time. which everyone has, he had no money, but he knew that thought was money; so he invested his thought in the now, knowing that it was not going to recede and vanish from sight; that was an investment: it would advance into his future.

Well it did. It's so advanced that he tells me now everything he touches turns to gold. Now he has three children; they come here every Sunday to Sunday school: he doesn't want his children to start with his stripes, so he wants them to feel what this Church gives. So every Sunday, Jimmie tells me many a Sunday he feels like taking off for the beach or up to the mountains with his wife, but he will not go because he wants his children to have an opportunity he didn't have. He says "My people were very religious, but they must have worshiped a very poor God, for they were steeped in poverty. So I just wouldn't go near the churches of my mother and my brothers and these people, because I couldn't conceive of such a God doing that to us; yet they never missed service. For when I found in this what I found here in this Science of Mind Church, I brought my children to Sunday School. Now this is what happened to them. Here God is love, and love surrounds them and they know nothing but love, that God is love. For one day my little girl, which is the youngest of the three, was quite sick, a beastly cold. and that night when the little boys said their prayers. these are the words they used 'Thank you God, that sister is perfect tomorrow.' They could not look at the little girl, sick as she was, and say 'Thank you God that sister is well now', but they said 'Thank you, God, that sister is perfect tomorrow'. Neville, it was a miracle. The next day that child was perfect; there wasn't the sign of a cold - a complete absence of all that we saw the night before, and these two little brothers simply gave thanks."

"Now, he wanted a watch. I wouldn't give him the watch. I could have bought a thousand watches for him. I want my little son to learn a law which I didn't know until recently. So he filled his mind with the possession of a watch, and he spoke of the watch as a 'live' watch - one that ticks, one that is alive, not a toy watch. So then he fills his mind with the possession of the watch. On his way to school he found a 'live' watch. Now he knows the working of law - that the complete acceptance of the state in consciousness must result in an externalization of the state accepted. So if he accepts the watch he need not turn to his earthly father, as the medium through which the watch will come. I don't want to think for one second he has to point to his mother or his father as the only channels through which his good will come. I want him to recognize an Infinite Father - the Father of US all - who gave to him as he gave to me everything that I will accept. I want my children to learn it as I have learned. Yes, I could shower him with gifts, but then he would look to me as the only channel through which it will come. That I must not accept. So you should see the little boys and little girls actually live by this law. God to them is love and the only reality and love surrounds them. So they never miss the Sunday School here."

Then he goes on to tell me all other wonderful things that have happened by the mere acceptance of this law. He said. "The getting of my car, this convertible Cadillac - I treated it loosely, I sat quietly in my living room and drove my Cadillac, and I simply treated for this loosely," he said, "I didn't put real effort into it, I accepted it and then when I decided to get it I simply put in three telephone calls and that day I was driving this car, Neville. Now everything happens just like that. Today, instead of going to my office and working in the office I work behind the scenes. I sit all day and I hear the report that is good from my employees; my entire office staff must tell me good news, the only thing I will allow myself to hear. I ride my car; I'm in the office; I am at home; I'm in the office but I am only hearing good news, and seldom do I go to the office physically to do office work, so I am behind the scenes only hearing good news. So I have completely forgotten the so-called pigment of skin and, Neville, honestly I can tell you today I feel that I am blessed beyond all men because I was born a negro. I am so proud to be born a negro; I am so proud I'm one."

And here is a story that will interest all of you; he said "I had some property to dispose of, I had certain things in investments for those who had money, and so I advertised it and a man called me on the wire. He saw the ad, and asked me if I was the gentleman, so I told him I was the one who had the property. The first thing he said to me, "I don't want any n***** property." Jimmie said, "I didn't answer, as if I hadn't even heard the word. If he wants to be prejudiced, he may be prejudiced, that's his right. He wants to be silly about it, that's his right. He can spend; he need not invest. So I said, "It is perfectly all right, sir, I have all kinds of property, I have all kinds of things for your investment." A week later he called me up and said, "Would you come and see me." He said, "I went to see him. When I got out of my car his knees almost buckled, for he didn't know a negro was coming to see him, and a negro walked up his stairs into his living room." He said within a matter of minutes he purchased $37,000 worth of mine that I had to offer. He said the first $25,000 that he bought he simply bought that to buy back his face, and then the remaining $12,000 he bought that because it was a very good investment. Well, since that time this gentleman has spent tens of thousands of dollars with me and constantly calls me to thank me because they are such wonderful investments"

In the lecture *The Spiritual Cause* on May 3, 1968 Neville said, "Now let me share a letter from a friend. It seems that when he first met him, his barber was the fourth man in a four-man shop. In case you are not familiar with a barber shop, the owner always has the first chair and, if it is a slow day he gets the customer. If he has finished when the second man comes in, the owner takes the second one also. If three more should come in, they will go to the different chairs, with the fourth barber being the last to receive a customer. One day my friend sat in his chair. As they talked, he discovered that the man was proud of his profession and desired to be the best barber in town. Hearing the desire expressed, my friend imagined the man had reached the top of his profession. Within a year the barber had bought the shop and had moved to the first chair!

Last month this barber told my friend of his desire to attend a hair styling contest in San Francisco. Realizing that no one goes to a contest unless he wants to win, my friend saw a trophy on the shelf near the door and heard the gentleman say he had won it. Last weekend three of the four men in the shop went to the contest and returned with four of the nine trophies given in the competition. The owner won a first and second place prize, with the two men who went with him each taking second. "Now" he said to me, "I have often heard you say from the platform: 'I will tell you before it takes place that when it does, you will believe me.' Now I am going to tell you, Neville, before it takes place, that he has already won the contest to be held in Southern California, for I have seen his trophy. Then he will go to Miami and win another trophy which will enable him to enter the international contest in Brussels, of which I have placed him as the winner." I know he will win, for every natural effect has a spiritual cause. My friend's imaginal act is the cause, and he will remember what he did and be blessed because of it."

Stories from the Audience

On June 20, 1969 in the lecture *The Ultimate Sense* Neville said, "One night a lady decided to test me by embracing a huge bouquet of roses. She caught the aroma of the rose and completely saturated herself with it, then she dropped the thought. This lady lived in the Waldorf Towers, and when she returned to her room the following evening she discovered three dozen roses had been placed there. It appeared that the Queen Mother was in New York City and had attended a banquet in her honor. Special roses were grown and [brought] there for her pleasure. The next day the maitre d' sent three dozen roses to this lady's room. She put her sense of smell to the test and within 24 hours her room was filled with roses.

I don't care who you are, I invite you to take the challenge. In the 13th chapter of 2 Corinthians you are asked this question: "Test yourself and see. Do you not realize that Jesus Christ is in you? Unless of course you fail to meet the test." Test God's power and God's wisdom, for encased in love you are testing the Christ seed within you. You can take anything and test this power. Do it just for the fun of it. Hold a long-stemmed rose in your hand. Touch its velvety petals and smell its heavenly aroma. Make a pledge to yourself that you will live by your imagination, for God has promised that you can assume a state and it will become a fact in his words: "Whatever you desire, believe you have received it and you will." It can't be stated any clearer than that. These are the words of an awakened man who is God, for every man who awakes in Jesus Christ is God, He who is forever extending himself."

Neville shared a story of a lady's brother who was in the army and was court-martialed and sentenced to six months of hard labor. In the lecture *Signs From Above* on June 24, 1968 he said, "In San Francisco, about ten years ago, I was teaching an audience of approximately one thousand, when a lady stood up and said: "My brother is in the army.

I do not know what he did, but I do know that he has been court-martialed and sentenced to six months of hard labor. Neville, if I believe you, can I not set my brother free?"

I said: "Yes, but only to the degree that you are self-persuaded that he is free." One week later this same lady stood up and told this story. "Believing you last week, when I returned home to my second floor apartment, I sat in my living room and imagined I heard the doorbell. Then I ran down the stairs, opened the front door and threw my arms around my brother. I rehearsed that scene over and over again until I could hear the doorbell ring, feel the banister in my right hand and my feet moving down the stairs. The doorknob became solidly real in my hand and I could see, touch, and feel my brother's presence before I stopped imagining.

"Last Wednesday evening, as I was dwelling upon my brother's return, the doorbell rang and I instantly knew it was he. I ran down the stairs, opened the door and there was my brother. He told me that the army had reviewed his case and changed their judgment, setting him free with an honorable discharge." This was a sign of the power of Christ operating in her. She believed the word and loved her brother deeply. Desiring her love to be free as the wind, she released it and in a way she could not rationally analyze, he whom she loved was set free.

You may think that was not right, but who is to say what is right and what is wrong? There are only two things that displease God. One is eating of the tree of knowledge of good and evil by judging what is right and what is wrong, and the other is the lack of faith in yourself!"

In the lecture *You Can Forgive Sin* on March 29, 1963 Neville said, "About three months ago a man sat in this audience, and he wrote me a sweet, wonderful letter which I received this morning. He expected a big bonus. He had worked hard with all the promise, and one who was never on the job, but by his estimate "one of the girl friends of the boss" - she got the big bonus. He, who had done all the work, got practically nothing. So, he and I agreed mentally that he would have the most wonderful job, with more money and everything. This is now going on April. It seemed a long while, but today he is on the job, with more money than he had – more than he expected – more responsibility and opportunity, and everything. I remained faithful to that letter I knew would come when he would write it. And all I did, I heard him tell me (mentally) what he would tell me were it true, and I never wavered."

On September 18, 1967 in the lecture *Yours For The Taking* Neville said, "Now, in the third letter a gentleman writes: "Having borrowed from the bank, every month when I sent in my payment I reduced the total amount in my record book. One day, as I was writing my check and recording its payment, I closed my eyes and saw two zeros under the balance due column. Then I gave a sigh of relief because the note was paid. For the next three months I persisted in seeing those double zeros and rejoicing in being debt-free. Then came an unexpected surprise! Our company paid us all a mid-year bonus which was so large I was able to pay all of my bills, including the bank loan, and deposit the rest in the bank."

Now I think this gentleman and I must be two peas in the same pod, because money seems to burn in his pocket, too. Instead of keeping the money in the bank as the rational mind would do, my friend began to think about how to spend it, so of course he found a way. He bought a tape recorder to bring and record my message!

To whom did my friend turn when he wanted the bank loan paid? He turned to God! He did not get down on his knees and ask some outside God to do it for him. He didn't go to church and consult a priest, rabbi or minister. He didn't contact a so-called truth teacher, but simply closed his eyes to the obvious and saw two zeros in the balance due column. Then for the first time in the history of his company a mid-year bonus was paid. This happened to him because of his use of the law, and his knowledge of who God is."

In the lecture *His Name* on February 26, 1963 Neville shared a story about a man who slept on the ground and smelled oil and became a millionaire. He said, "Now here is a true story which I heard this last Saturday. I am not a member of the Turf Club, but I go occasionally when I am invited and someone takes me. So last Saturday I and my wife were taken to the Turf Club. I was introduced to this little man who sat just one row below. Strange, weird little fellow, and then they told me his story. He had come here penniless from Kentucky. How he got the money necessary to buy a small little plot of land, I do not know, that was not told me; but he bought a small little plot of land in Ventura County. He wanted to have oil, so he would sleep on the land itself. He didn't build some little shack – he slept right on the ground. With his head to the ground he would hear oil coming in, he would smell oil, and he would come home sometimes in the morning at 6 A.M. and his wife was distraught. "What has happened to you?" He was sleeping on the land bringing it in.

Today the man – I would say he is ten years my senior, which is 68, pushing 70 – he has no financial problems. He has given away fortunes. He is worth over six million, so he told me himself, but now he has another problem, and he has forgotten the name of God. His present problem is boredom. He goes to the track five days a week, Tuesday through Saturday. If he drops ten thousand, it's no problem, if he drops twenty thousand, that's no problem. But he is bored and he is not physically well, and he doesn't remember how he brought oil into being by the name of God. When he put his head on that earth and began to listen, who was listening? If you would say to him: "What are you doing?"

"I am smelling oil." That's what he would say. You have called the name of God. "I am smelling oil. I am hearing oil," is what he would say. He brought it all in, but he doesn't remember the name of God. Now he is saying: "I am unwell." He is blaspheming the name of God. You are told: "The man who blasphemes the name of God, stone him to death." The stone is "showing the facts of life," so he is showing the facts of life. "You aren't feeling well, are you?" So you see all the things in the world wrong with him, and you tell him. These are the stones, but he has forgotten and those around him don't know. He once used the name of God wisely and brought wealth into this world. He could bring health into this world if he would use the name of God."

In the lecture *The Law* on November 20, 1959 Neville said, "Here is this lady driving east on Sunset and she comes to a stop at Laurel Canyon. A bus is to her right, and then she sees this little elderly lady in gray who is running diagonally across the street through traffic, trying to catch that bus. The bus driver sees her but he pulls out leaving her on the street. The lady, who gave me this story, told me that she felt compassion for this elderly lady, but she was not in a lane where she could give her a lift; she had to pull out with her line when the light changed. She said to herself, "I will give that lady a lift just the same." So in Imagination, she opens her car door and lets her in.

Then still in her Imagination, she hears the lady tell her that she is meeting some friends a few blocks away and if she had to wait for another bus she is afraid they would not wait for her. The lady in the car carried on this imaginary conversation and it took maybe a half a minute until she felt satisfied about it. Four blocks ahead, as she again stopped for a light, someone tapped on the car window, and here stands a breathless little elderly with gray hair dressed in gray. My friend lowered the window and the little lady said "I have missed my bus. Can you give me a lift? Friends are waiting for me and when they see I do not get off the bus they may go on and leave me." My friend let her get into the car and then six blocks further the little lady said. "There are my friends!" and thanks the driver and gets out.

Now here is a lady whom I say is awake. And may I tell you that in Heaven there was joy because one called a sinner (we are all sinners, for we are all missing the mark, and the mark is to awaken) has discovered that the whole world is responsive to what we are thinking. She could not actually give the first little lady a lift so she did it in Imagination, and then she sees this other elderly lady and gives her a lift. Here she is enacting her imaginary drama, and four blocks later when the dream is completed this little ole lady taps at her car window. In her imagination she gave a lift to a little gray haired lady dressed in gray. Does it matter if it was the lady behind at the last bus stop or this lady dressed in gray? Everyone is responding to what we are doing in our Imagination. There is no outside world that is really alive. It depends, for its aliveness, on the activity of man who is a living soul. Man named the animals, the birds, the trees, – everything. God became man as a living soul, but He had to forget He was God to become man, and now man has to become a life-giving spirit, where he knows that everything is an imaginal activity.

Here, at that corner where the first part of this little drama took place, half of those who witnessed it would bawl out the bus driver for not waiting for the old lady, and the other half would say she was a fool for running into the street. This lady in the car could have reacted like that, for the dreamer does not know that he is dreaming. It is only when we awake they know they are causing the dream, or even had a dream. The lady in the car saw only someone who had failed to realize an objective, so she enacted a scene for her, implying she had realized it. And four blocks later she meets a little old lady who says to her the exact words she had heard in her Imagination. Her Imaginary dream unfolds in detail. An awakened dream is crystallized in the world. "Real are the dreams of gods, as they slowly pass their pleasure in a long immortal dream." When man completely awakens he dreams his pleasure and everything responds while he dreams it."

Neville shared two stories in the lecture *Walk By Faith* on November 6, 1967 he said, "Another lady went to Stern's Department Store in New York City, saying to herself: "Neville says I can have anything I want if I will imagine and believe in my imaginal act." Having no money, this lady walked over to the hat department, took off her hat and tried on a new one. Walking around the area, she admired herself in front of all the mirrors, but when she returned, her hat was gone. When she described it to the sales lady, she learned that her hat had been sold! The section manager was called in, and he told her to take any hat she wanted, compliments of Sterns. She liked the one she had been wearing, so she left the store with her new hat on her head, and she hadn't paid a dime for it.

Here is another story of a similar nature. This lady's profession was that of being a lady of the evening. She attended all of my meetings, and one day she said to me; "You know, Neville, the strangest thing happened. You told me that I could have anything I wanted if I simply imagined it.

One day I saw a beautiful hat in the window of a department store on Broadway. It was $18, but I loved it so I imagined wearing the hat. As I walked up the street I kept looking at my reflection in the shop windows, seeing that hat on my head. Arriving home, I imagined placing the new hat in the closet instead of my old one. Every day, for the next week or ten days, as I put on my old hat, I imagined it was the new one. Then one day a friend called and asked me to come see her. While there, she brought out a hat box and said; 'I must have been insane when I bought this hat. I wouldn't wear it to a dog fight; yet strangely enough I feel it would look lovely on you.' She opened the box and brought out, not a hat, but the hat, the very hat I had seen in the window and worn in my imagination." Then she asked: "Neville, why didn't God give me the money to buy the hat myself, instead of giving it to me in this manner?"

Knowing her profession, I said, "Ann, do you owe any rent?" and she replied, "Yes, two weeks." "What do you pay, about $17.50 per week?" "Yes." "So you owe $35. What price hats do you usually buy? Three or four dollar ones? Have you ever bought a $17 hat?" "Never." "Then tell me honestly. If, when you were looking at the hat, you had seen a $100 bill on the ground, would you have brought the hat?" She said "No." Then I said, "No matter how much money God might have given you, you still would not have bought the hat, so someone else had to buy it for you, and they did."

I have bought clothes, brought them home, and wondered what possessed me to buy them. I did it because someone was treading in the winepress elsewhere. Someone imagined a suit of clothes, so I went to my tailor, chose the cloth, and paid for the suit. But when I brought it home, my wife wouldn't let me bring it into the house. Then a friend who wanted something just like it contacted me and got the suit. He was treading the winepress while I paid for the suit."

Also by Jeff Johnson

The Mystical Experiences of Neville Goddard

Neville Goddard (1905-1972) emerged as a prominent figure in metaphysics, captivating audiences as both an insightful author and a captivating lecturer. His profound teachings explored the power of imagination and consciousness in shaping reality, leaving an enduring legacy in personal transformation.

In researching over 300 of his lectures, this book shares Neville's mystical stories of his visions throughout his life.

"One day, when someone said, "He just has hallucinations; he's standing up there telling us a bunch dreams that he has; they're just all illusion," and he heard somebody say something like that, and he said, "This body disintegrate in your presence if what I'm telling you isn't the absolute Truth." He was calling on such Power to destroy him if it weren't absolutely true. So you know you can believe Neville; if he said it, you know it was true."

"Freedom On The Beach" Lecture By Freedom Barry

Don't miss out!

Visit the website below and you can sign up to receive emails whenever Jeff Johnson publishes a new book. There's no charge and no obligation.

https://books2read.com/r/B-A-GLBZ-GARKC

BOOKS 2 READ

Connecting independent readers to independent writers.

Milton Keynes UK
Ingram Content Group UK Ltd.
UKHW020730290923
429627UK00017B/994